# Laurel Queen's
## Claim to Fame


## By
## Andrew Hoyle

Copyright ©PRIDE OF PLACE PUBLISHING

This Edition First published in 1994
by
Pride of Place Publishing

10 9 8 7 6 5 4 3 2 1

British Library Cataloguing in Publication Data.
A catalogue record for this book is available from
the British Library.

ISBN 1 874645 14 0

Typeset by
READ THIS PUBLISHING,

Printed in Great Britain by
BPC Wheatons Ltd, Exeter

PRIDE OF PLACE PUBLISHING LTD
UNIT 9, CBTC,
EUXTON LANE, CHORLEY
LANCASHIRE, PR7 6TE

# CONTENTS

Foreword
Acknowledgements
Dedication

# FOREWORD BY JACK BERRY

Laurel Queen was one of the most popular females ever to grace the turf and will be remembered for her proven ability on the track. She was 100% professional, not a bit complicated, genuine, tough and consistent.

I had the privilege of training her at Cockerham all her working life. From day one when she was officially named Laurel Queen, in the yard she was only known as "Queenie" or "The Queen", a name she admirably lived up to. For my own part and by the amount of letters we received from her many fans may I say a big thank you.

I wish you well old girl at stud and look forward very much to training your offspring. I will tell them all about you, and what Andrew has written in human terms means "Laurel Queen - This is Your Life".

# Acknowledgements

Grateful thanks to:

The Berry family and stable staff

John Carroll
Other Jockeys to win on Laurel Queen:
Gary Carter,
Pat Eddery,
Nicky Carlisle,
Gary Bardwell
and
Richard Quinn.

Mary Reveley
Geoff Lewis
Secretary Pat
Racing Post
Sporting Life

## Dedication

To my wife Pat, ace secretary of Laurel Racing Club and devout fan of Laurel Queen

# CHAPTER 1

## WHAT'S IN A NAME

Turf historians tell us that the Derby could have been called the Bunbury had a toss of a coin gone the other way. It was virtually a toss-up whether the yearling filly we purchased in the autumn of 1989 became Laurel Queen...or Kestrel Forboxes!

One of our first-year club members, Reg Brooks, offered to put some money into the club funds if we named one of our horses after his box-manufacturing company, Kestrel.

Secretary Pat had taken a shine to our yearling filly by Viking, out of Prima Bella, when we first visited her at the Cockerham stables. That swayed me into ensuring that the filly carried the "Laurel" name. Consequently, I invited Reg Brooks to put his company's name to the other yearling we had purchased, a colt by Seymour Hicks, out of Dance Mistress. Maybe we can claim to be among the pioneers of racehorse sponsorship. At the time, I checked with Weatherbys to ensure this was in order, and they said it was all right as a private arrangement.

Laurel Queen was among a batch of yearlings obtained by Adrian Maxwell - acting on Jack Berry's behalf - at the Fairyhouse Sales in Ireland. I bought her unseen for 7,800 guineas. While her sire, Viking, was unfashionable, he was a son of the great Northern Dancer. And Laurel Queen's dam, Prima Bella, had bred winners, including a couple trained by Jack. I am always impressed by a dam that has bred winners.

Laurel Queen was certainly to do her bit for the family in her four-year racing career. Two days after Laurel Queen won at Ayr in July, 1992, her two years younger half-brother, Finmental (pronounced F-inmental, to the embarrassment of Weatherbys and the Jockey Club), carried 9st 7lb to victory in an Ayr nursery, with the vanquished including Mistertopogigo, who was foiled of a hat-trick. Finmental was trained by Alan Bailey, who won two Ayr races for our club with the mare, Rose Glen.

After bringing Laurel Queen over from Ireland, Jack sent her (along with the other yearlings purchased at Fairyhouse), to spend a few weeks with Stephen Wiles at Emley Moor in Yorkshire. Jack explained: "You have to be careful when there are horses in training, and others are brought into the yard from the sales. If you have them housed elsewhere for a while, it is a precaution against the possible spread of a virus."

Not that Laurel Queen was to prove prone to virus problems after joining the Cockerham team to be trained for racecourse action as a two-year-old in the 1990 season. Nor did she experience any serious setbacks due to illness or injury in her four years of racing.

Reflecting on her career, Jack said: "I can say, hand on heart, that I have never trained a tougher filly. If there was ever anything wrong with her, then her recovery time would be very fast."

"There was nothing complicated about her. She was a pleasure to train. She had a little streak in her that might be interpreted as impatience - like someone who doesn't suffer fools gladly. She would be perfectly happy to go down to the gallops and work over six or seven furlongs. But she would want to get

12

on with it.  It would be no use giving her a couple of turns, and waiting around.  For that reason, I liked her to be taken out of the parade ring, and down to the start of a race, as quickly as possible.  She was like that all her life.  Laurel Queen was her own woman."

Why was she able to win so many races?  Jack puts that down to playing things low-key early in her career.  "We won a seller with her, and then a second one.  Then came the small step up to a claimer.  She was brought along nice and quietly, no big steps or aspirations."

"If we had tried to win good handicaps early on, there would have been no record number of wins at the end of her career.  The attempts in big handicaps, like the Lincoln, and Victoria Cup, were justified after other avenues had been explored.  But for injury ending her career, there's no telling how long she could have continued or how many more races she could have won."

"Laurel Queen was always true and genuine.  She gave 100 per cent, and loved racing.  John Carroll struck up a tremendous partnership with her.  He loved Laurel Queen and would have gone through fire and water to ride her.  If Laurel Queen was ever ridden by another jockey it was because I was duty-bound to send John somewhere else on the day."

Paying tribute to her during Sky TV coverage at Lingfield, Ian Carnaby said:  "She is a wonderful mare, and the great thing about her is that in loads of those wins she has come under quite strong pressure.  She wouldn't know how to chuck it, and it is a sight to see as she battles on.  It is a fantastic story."

Geoff Lewis, who trained the three-year-old filly, Plan Ahead, to pip Laurel Queen for the Channel Four Trophy in 1992, said: "When I won a mile claimer with Plan Ahead at Nottingham, in April, I could hardly have visualised that she would end the season with eight successes. After Nottingham, Plan Ahead won an apprentices' handicap at Warwick, then completed her hat-trick at Lingfield. Her fourth win was achieved in an Epsom claimer at the Derby meeting."

"We began to think of ourselves as Channel Four Trophy contenders - with Laurel Queen an obvious threat. Plan Ahead won another claimer at Sandown to take her tally to five. Laurel Queen was still notching the wins, but we finally came out on top when Plan Ahead completed a hat-trick of handicap wins at Folkestone, Goodwood and Ascot, to enable us to take the Trophy 8-7."

"A filly as consistent and progressive as Plan Ahead doesn't come along very often. Laurel Queen has displayed similar qualities in compiling her post-war record for a filly or mare. And if that record is ever broken, I doubt if it will be within the space of four seasons, the time in which it was achieved by Laurel Queen."

With 22 wins to her credit, after adding six to her career tally in the 1993 season, Laurel Queen was looking a picture and raring to go again, when disaster struck during her preparation for the next campaign.

Jo Webster, who was looking after Laurel Queen, and rode her in home work during preparation for the 1994 season, said: "She was stronger than ever and tremendously well. I rode her in a gallop, and she quickened up to go past the others, who included Cee Jay Ay, the winner of the Spring Mile a year before."

Jo, like everyone else at Cockerham, was convinced that it had been a big mistake not to enter her for the Lincoln.

Jack had been cursing me for deciding against making another Lincoln bid. And I was kicking myself, because she looked magnificent! "I have never known her do so well during the winter," Jack said. Then the 'phone call came with the bad news that Laurel Queen had knocked herself on a hind leg. "She's lame at the moment, but I don't think it's anything serious," Jack said. A week later, Laurel Queen was pleasing the vet by responding to treatment. However, the injury subsequently became infected and resulted in damage to a tendon. The tendon was forced down and affected her stride.

After a consultation with the vet, who was of the opinion that she would be unlikely to race again, it was decided that Laurel Queen should be retired to stud.

Jack said: "When she sustained the injury, we didn't fully appreciate the problem at first. We thought that when the swelling subsided, she would soon be on the mend. After all, she was as tough as old boots - just like Lester Piggott! It was the end of an era, and we all miss seeing her in action. I'll look forward to training any of Laurel Queen's offspring. Another one like her will do!"

We made inquiries regarding Laurel Queen's possible coverage by Zoman at the National Stud, but the stallion was failing to get mares in foal. We were offered the former Henry Cecil - trained Keen as an alternative.

Keen is by Sharpen Up, the sire of Selkirk, who had covered our four-year-old sprinter, Laurel Delight, at Newmarket's Lanwades Stud. Whereas Laurel Delight was able to return to

Cockerham in-foal, to successfully resume racing for a restricted spell, Laurel Queen failed pregnancy tests in three attempts by Keen. We then decided to wait until the 1995 covering season, and arrange a nomination for her with a different sire, although we are not blaming Keen for her drawing a blank. He had been getting other mares in foal.

Laurel Queen will have to get a move on in the "maternity stakes" if she's to prove a chip off her late mother, Prima Bella, who sadly was put down in 1994 at the age of 22. Prima Bella bred seven winners, starting with Erlinda, who was born in 1978. Prior to Laurel Queen, Jack had trained Prima Bella's produce, No More The Fool and Monteros Boy. The other winners out of Prima Bella were Barefoot Rogue, Get Set Lisa and Finmental.

Prima Bella was owned by Edmund Lonergan, of Fennor House, Urlingford, Thurles, Co. Tipperary. Describing Prima Bella as a "wonderful mare," Mr Lonergan recalled: "She had two barren years, which I put down to her foaling No More The Fool. He was huge, and very hard to foal."

"Prima Bella certainly produced a tough one in Laurel Queen, who spent much of her early life with her front legs up against an 8ft wall. Despite all her rearing up, she could look after herself. I followed her career with great interest, and I'm proud to have been associated with her."

The last in the line of Prima Bella's offspring is a filly by Fayruz, foaled in 1992. Mr Lonergan intends to keep the filly for breeding, so Laurel Queen's half-sister can help to maintain the family's success story.

# CHAPTER 2

## NOT A "SHARP" SORT

Jack Berry is renowned for producing two-year-olds trained to know their job first time out. The best of the Berry bunch of juveniles will usually have been introduced to racecourse action during the first couple of months of the season. If you own a two-year-old in this stable, and it's a long time coming out, that's a bad sign. Consequently, we wondered what we were in for when Laurel Queen didn't make her debut until July 2, in the 1990 season.

The Wragby Maiden Stakes, over five furlongs, at Pontefract, was the launching pad. The going was officially given as "firm." I would have described it as "hard," and not really an ideal surface for introducing a two-year-old. However, Jack was confident that she would cope with it. He commented: "Whatever her running here, she will improve." When John Carroll brought Laurel Queen out onto the course for the down-hill canter to the start she looked a lot greener than the Pontefract grass. Jack had obviously found her anything but a precocious type. She was taking it all in, looking at the crowd, and throwing her head about in a way that was to become characteristic. She had seven opponents, and started a 9-2 chance. If she was slow going down to the start, she was even slower out of the starting stalls - and not in much of a hurry for the first two furlongs. There was going to be no debut success for Laurel Queen. But it wasn't all gloom and doom. Getting the hang of things from Ponte's home turn, she made late progress to finish fourth, just over seven lengths adrift of Mostimus.

Jack Berry and John Carroll both thought that Laurel Queen's debut was satisfactory...as it had looked to us watching from the stands. Our each-way bets were down but there would be another day. "We'll find a maiden race for her in the near future," Jack said.

Only eight days later, Laurel Queen was back on the Ponte beat for a similar event - but over six furlongs.

Once again, we backed her each-way at S.P but there was more support for her in the betting market than we had anticipated and she started 5-2 second favourite. The ground was just as rock-hard as at the previous meeting and again Laurel Queen didn't seem to like it. She did get off to a better start, but was always going to play either second or third fiddle as the heavily gambled-on favourite, Bijoux D'Or, made sweet music for her supporters. We were very thrilled to see Laurel Queen improve on her debut run to the extent of finishing third after a photo for places with Horstay. "She will definitely win a claimer or seller over six or seven furlongs," Jack said. As we wanted a winner or two to keep our Laurel club members happy, I told Jack that we should set our stall out to win a couple of sellers. A youngster isn't allowed to win more than twice in sellers. We shopped around for a suitable seller and found one at Yarmouth on July 18.

Earlier in the season, I had claimed a two-year-old, Classic Ring, after she had finished third in a Nottingham seller. Classic Ring was running at Catterick, half-an-hour before Laurel Queen's Yarmouth race. Both horses were fancied, so I took the easier option and went to Catterick to save travelling time.

Classic Ring was trained by Tommy Fairhurst and we had

18

booked Richard Quinn to ride. In a field of nine, Jack Berry opposed with Bold Spark. The dry weather had continued and the Catterick going was fast. Classic Ring coped with the conditions admirably. Richard had her out of the stalls like a flash and she was always in command over the seven furlongs, winning by three lengths from Peter Easterby's well-fancied Whimbrel. Classic Ring started at 6-1 but we had obtained 8-1 in the ring. There was a bonus too, with "no bid" at the selling race auction. Now our thoughts turned to Laurel Queen. Could she do the business down at Yarmouth?

Jack Berry was at Catterick. He congratulated us on Classic Ring's victory, adding: "Tommy turned that horse out fit to run for its life."

I found a position to watch on SIS as Laurel Queen, partnered by Pat Eddery made her bid to land our double. Her chance in a seller was obvious following a couple of promising runs in better company. Consequently, she was 11-10 favourite at "the off." Prominent from the start over Yarmouth's straight seven furlongs, Pat allowed her to take the lead approaching halfway. Never having been out in front before in a race, it wasn't surprising that Laurel Queen should "wander" about, but she was always holding the opposition and we urged her on in great excitement as she won by two lengths from Green Enterprise. We had arranged to "buy in" Laurel Queen, but this was our lucky day and again there was no bid.

For our Laurel members attending Catterick or Yarmouth, or indeed for those throughout the country following the fortunes of our horses by whatever means, it was a truly memorable occasion. In our first year, the club's winning tally was now three. We had got off the mark when Fleet Footed, trained by Mary Reveley, and ridden by Bob Hodge, won a Conditional

Jockeys' Claiming Hurdle at Catterick, in February. Not bad, a winner from only our second runner - and at 8-1.

"I told you there would be no bid for Laurel Queen," Jack said. "Not many people are interested in buying fillies out of sellers and claimers. Now we can look for that second seller." But after our "Lord Mayor's Show" of a racing day, the "Muckcart" was to follow on Laurel Queen's next appearance.

# CHAPTER 3

## LAUREL QUEEN'S EYESORE

It's said that the stewards dine until half past three and then they start to have their tea. They must have been preoccupied in passing the port when Laurel Queen flopped, as favourite, at Redcar, then bounced back to winning form at Thirsk, with no questions asked. A glance at Laurel Queen's credentials was all that punters required to make her 6-4 favourite for Redcar's Fine Leg Selling Stakes. But her supporters must have thought this was just not cricket when she turned in a remarkably wayward run to finish only ninth in a field of 12. Our only pre-race worry had been Laurel Queen's No. 1 draw, which put her on the outside of the field, and in the middle of the course. Laurel Queen was slowly away, then gradually hung to the left, with John Carroll unable to prevent her from drifting to the far side of the track, where she raced alone. Her chance had gone by the half-way stage over the straight seven furlongs. We could only wait and wonder in disappointment until John reported back to us. However, on Laurel Queen's return, we could see that all wasn't well with her. There was a discharge from her right eye and this was causing her some distress. John wasn't sure whether she had knocked herself while in the stalls. Jack wondered if it was an eye-problem that might recur. He reasoned: "The best thing to do is get the eye healed-up, win another seller, then think about letting her go, just in case the problem does recur." We now came to the conclusion that Laurel Queen had hung to the left during the race because she was running away from her "blind eye." I consoled our club members by pointing out to them that they could benefit from this situation next time. "On the face of it, this is a disappointing run, but you know the reason for it, and provided the eye problem responds to treatment, she could start at a decent price next time out."

It's an ill wind, as they say, and the outcome of the Redcar race certainly blew Mary Reveley some good. She won with Kagram Queen, whose owner-breeder had promised her a "monkey" the first time the filly was successful. We waited patiently for news of Laurel Queen's well-being during the days following Redcar, and Jack began to give us favourable vibes. Despite the Redcar reverse, the club was doing well to the extent that the "Sporting Life" described us as "enjoying a purple patch."

Our two-year-old Kestrel Forboxes made a promising debut at Pontefract, followed by placed runs at Thirsk and Carlisle. He then won his maiden at Bath, where little could be seen of the race until Kestrel Forboxes came out of the mist ahead of Teanarco and 16 others. Lindsay Charnock said: "He was fast out of the stalls, and I never saw another horse after that. It was even difficult to see the winning post."

Jack persuaded me to run Kestrel Forboxes in York's Jervaulx Selling Stakes, which opened the Magnet Cup card. "You'll be able to stand at the front and buy him back. You'll be in control. It's less risky than running him in a claimer." I agreed, and intended to have a good punt on our horse against the odds-on chance, La Maraquita. When we arrived at York, La Maraquita had been withdrawn, and Kestrel Forboxes was 11-4 on. He won in a canter by 15 lengths prompting the commentator to say: "You won't find many races at York won as easily as this." The bidding at the selling race auction topped £8,000 before we could buy him in. Our profit on the race was only £502.26.

Just over five weeks elapsed after the Redcar race before
Laurel Queen was declared fit for action again. We still didn't
know whether the eye problem had been caused by injury. Still
seeking that second success in a seller, we decided to go for the
Mel Brittain Selling Stakes over seven furlongs, at Thirsk.
Jack produced Laurel Queen looking the proverbial picture.
The ground was good, and she seemed far more at ease going
to the post than she had on firm terrain. With John Carroll
required to ride Jack's runners at Chester, Gary Carter was on
board Laurel Queen. In a field of 15, the majority of them no-
hopers, Laurel Queen seemed fairly priced at 7-2. Drawn in
stall No. 7, Gary Carter found her a little slow into her stride.
Making good headway from the rear, towards the outside,
Laurel Queen quickened up to win comfortably from Friday
Fourball. This was very pleasing in several aspects. We had
Laurel Queen fit and well again. She had demonstrated that
she could win either by making the running or coming from
behind. Then to put some icing on the cake, we heard the auc-
tioneer call, "no bid" at the selling race auction.

Mel Brittain presented me with the race trophy, a silver
tankard. There must have been many punters put off backing
Laurel Queen at Thirsk because of her bad run when favourite
at Redcar. Backers were not to know about her eye problem.
It's often said in such circumstances: "That's not the same
horse." Of course, there was only one Laurel Queen. We did-
n't have a lookalike. In all my racing years, I was only once
convinced that I had seen a ringer in action. It happened at
Devon and Exeter (as the venue was called then) and Newton
Abbot meetings within the space of four days. A horse that had
been running reasonably well in novice hurdles was dropped in
class to contest a very poor Devon seller. It was so "easy" in the
on-course betting market that it was all too obviously not going

to win. The horse trailed home like a cripple. That was on a Saturday. On the following Wednesday, the horse was back in much better company in a Newton Abbot novices' hurdle. This time the "Devon cripple" produced a run between the last two hurdles with the jockey (the same top-class pilot as at Devon) reminding me of Pat Glennon winning the Derby so stylishly on Sea Bird II. The Newton Abbot price was 100-8. Later, news filtered through that the horse had been substantially backed off course. It happened in the ringing (I mean the swinging) sixties. I was there!

The Thirsk success meant that was our lot in sellers while Laurel Queen was a two-year-old. "We'll go for a claimer now," said Jack, ever-watchful for the next winning opportunity. What had he said about letting her go? We would certainly have been keen to retain her had anyone put in bids at Thirsk. Her pace suggested she was better than a plater. After seeing Laurel Queen turn in such a silk-smooth display on Thirsk's good ground, it was back to the hard stuff when she contested a Carlisle claimer a couple of weeks later. I felt for our filly, competing on ground officially described as: "Firm - with hard patches." The seven furlongs of the Cumbria course is much stiffer than the Thirsk seven. Consequently, it was against her that she now decided to take a strong hold. After running freely, and taking the lead with a quarter of a mile to go, the uphill final furlong found her wanting, and she faded into fourth place behind Station Express. John Carroll thus remained out of luck on her. And he missed out again when Laurel Queen returned to winning form at Yarmouth eight days later.

John's pal, Gary Carter, also missed the chance to add to his Thirsk success on Laurel Queen. John's services were required at Ayr, where he drew a blank. Gary turned down the ride on

Laurel Queen, preferring to partner the Newmarket horse, Lady Baraka, who was reckoned to be "the business." Gary Carter's agent also booked rides for Gary Bardwell...so opportunity knocked for the "Angry Ant." And what a super-sub he turned out to be!

After keeping Laurel Queen tucked away in mid-field, and out of the teeth of a gale-force wind, for the first five furlongs, Gary Bardwell had Laurel Queen in command inside the final two. From there on, it was eat your heart out Gary Carter... making vain attempts to get the gambled-on Lady Baraka (backed from 12-1 to 11-2) on terms. Neither was Laurel Queen lacking support. Backed from 8-1 to sixes, she landed the bets by one length. Jack Berry's old mate, former Newmarket trainer, Gerry Blum, who was looking after the saddling, and often helps out with Jack's southern runners, thought that by being kept shielded from the wind for much of the race, this had helped Laurel Queen's cause enormously. Our cause was also helped when there was no claim for Laurel Queen. Putting in "friendly claims" to retain horses can be an expensive business. I had a £50 bet with Jack Berry that there WOULD be a claim for Laurel Queen. I was much relieved when there was NOT...and happy to lose that particular bet.

Given her chance in a 17-strong Wolverhampton nursery next time out Laurel Queen ran well to be edged out of fourth place behind Maggie Siddons, trained by Barnstaple-based, John Hill.

One more run on the all-weather at Southwell told us that Laurel Queen was "over the top" for the season. She led then faded in the home straight. Three wins was a nice contribution to our first club year. Our other youngster, Kestrel Forboxes, had also weighed in with three wins, and the successes of

Classic Ring and Fleet Footed gave us a club tally of eight. Not bad for starters. But we didn't know that the best was yet to come from Laurel Queen.

# CHAPTER 4

## SLIM-LINE SUCCESS

LAUREL QUEEN was produced fit enough to start her three-year-old campaign with a Warwick win, but she only just held on over the seven furlongs to gain a short head verdict over Richard Hannon's Bid For Elegance. When Laurel Queen was subsequently beaten at Thirsk, we looked back on her Warwick success as a win achieved while still a shade short of her best. John Carroll had missed out on Laurel Queen's two-year-old victories due to his services being required elsewhere. He was in the saddle at Warwick, and also when Laurel Queen went on from Thirsk to recapture winning form at Carlisle, where her starting price of 11-4 looked tremendous value as she stormed home 10 lengths clear of what seemed moderate claiming race opposition. John Carroll reported: "She really bounced off the ground." The going was officially described as "good to firm" and Laurel Queen now seemed happy enough on fast terrain.

There had been a no claims bonus at Warwick, and once again we got away with it at Carlisle. During this period, Jack Berry would deride my inclination to make out a "friendly" claim form and have it at the ready in case there was any last minute claim submitted. Jack took the view that because he neither claimed horses, or bought them out of sellers, people wouldn't go after his. But times were gradually a changing. From being something of a "closed shop," the claiming race scene was becoming more of an open market.

For the benefit of the uninitiated in claiming race matters, horses are entered in such events according to the owner's stipulated price, and carry a weight associated to that price. The terms of the race may state allowances: For each £1,000 below the maximum claiming price of £10,000, 1lb (minimum claiming price £3,000).

The race conditions for claiming events vary greatly, and the top claiming price could be £20,000. Sometimes, the weight allowance is 2lb for each £1,000 below the maximum. In a nutshell, the higher the price put on the horse, the more the weight to be carried. Prior to a claiming race rule change in April 1994, a claim could be put in at, or above, the stipulated price. This applied to any horse competing in the race. The owner of a contestant could submit a "friendly" claim if not wishing to lose the horse. Claims were submitted after the race until the clerk of the scales decided that "time is up." The claims were then scrutinised, with the highest taking the horses involved. Under the new rule, claims can only be made at the stipulated price. If two or more claims are made for the same horse, a ballot decides the outcome. Numbered balls are used...as in the FA Cup draw. A successful claim is subject to a 15 per cent buyer's premium.

Laurel Queen continued her 1991 campaign by going on from her Carlisle claiming success to contest a similar seven furlongs event at Doncaster.

From an unfavourable No. 6 draw in a Doncaster field of 19, Laurel Queen did well to dispute the lead with two furlongs to go, but she finally had to settle for third place behind the better drawn Fizz Time and Northern Rising. The filly was a 5-1 chance and her each-way supporters saw her snatch the minor place by a short head from Alton Bay. It was a satisfactory effort as the opposition was appreciably stronger than at

Carlisle.

A fortnight later, we had Laurel Queen heading for Hamilton in another claiming race attempt. This time, the distance was a mile, but John Carroll thought that it would be best to try and make all the running, provided Laurel Queen was well away from the stalls. A policy was gradually emerging of letting Laurel Queen run her races according to how she came out of the stalls. She was eager to be off on this occasion, and soon had her nine Hamilton opponents strung out.

There was a semblance of a challenge to her from the second favourite, Stairway To Heaven, with two furlongs to go, but Laurel Queen surged away to win by seven lengths as Dust Dthrone stayed on to finish second. With Laurel Queen starting 11-8 favourite, she was resoundingly roared on to success. But when the elation of victory subsided, the hazards of claiming race involvement became all too evident. In the excitement of the occasion, I neglected to be as diligent as usual in keeping any eye on the claiming situation. By the time that I reached the weighing room, and started to write out a friendly claim, the clerk of the scales was signalling that I was too late. A claim had been submitted at the last minute, and that was instantly followed by a friendly claim on behalf of Dust Dthrone, trained by Lyn Siddall. What a relief when the claims were opened and we had got away with it. Lucky for some, but not for Lyn Siddall. After seeing Dust Dthrone, a 33-1 chance, turn in a promising seasonal debut, Lyn feared there could be a claim for her colt.

Accordingly, she tendered a friendly claim on behalf of Dust Dthrone but was surprised when the rival claim turned out to be for her other horse in the race, Alkabar, who had finished last. The claim had cost Lyn money...plus a horse. Later that day, Lyn was able to "do a deal" with the claimee, Col. Montieth, for the return of Alkabar, whose owners didn't want to lose the horse. Asked how much the whole episode cost her, Lyn said: "I don't want to remember, but it was a lot."

Laurel Queen had hit the Hamilton opposition for her sixth success and the "Superform" publication described her as: "A specialist over seven furlongs, but stays a stiff mile: acts on good and fast ground, and does well fresh: loves to force the pace: a very tough and genuine filly." The mid-May outing having taken little out of her, we returned to perusing the Racing Calendar for a suitable target towards the end of the month. We liked the look of the one mile Levy Board Apprentice Stakes at Carlisle on May 30.

A few days after Hamilton, Jack reported that Laurel Queen was "bouncing" and raring to go again. He agreed that the Carlisle event was attractive, although we didn't really regard our filly as an ideal mount for an apprentice. While she was a professional during a race, she could be a bit tricky to handle between the parade ring and going into the stalls. At least, we would be given some welcome respite from the worries of the claiming scene. At Carlisle, we were to find problems of a completely different kind!

# CHAPTER 5

## SURPRISES COME IN THREES

Very little surprises me after spending the best part of a life-
time involved in racing. However, I can well recall a trio of
Turf happenings that I would have to term "shocks."

The 5-1 on defeat of Laurel Queen at Carlisle on May 30, 1991,
still leaves us feeling the occasional twinge from chronic shell-
shock.

Another major surprise came with the announcement that
Robert Sangster was to make Michael Dickinson his flat racing
trainer. I was equally amazed by the Michael Stoute stable's
decision - obviously with the blessing of his holiness the Aly
Khan - to run Shergar in the 1981 St Leger.

During his days as an amateur rider, and then professional
jockey, and later as assistant trainer to his father Tony, before
taking over the training licence himself, Michael Dickinson
had never been the slightest bit interested in flat racing.

While he was at Gisburn and Harewood, I would be in regular
contact with him about the stable's jumpers, and he'd be happy
to talk about them in detail and mull over prospects of form
and winning chances. But ask him about the stable's flat horses - his father kept one or two for summer interest - and he did-
n't want to know. "You'll have to see what father thinks,"
would be the reply. Consequently, I had to be amazed that
such "credentials" brought him the Sangster job. I wasn't sur-

prised that Michael took some time to sort things out at his new Manton base. When this perfectionist did get everything organised and prepared for racecourse activity, I was apprehensive about the quality of horses he was asked to start with. They seemed more a bunch of Hamilton hopes than potential classic contenders. Maybe Sangster had thought that Dickinson could become another Vincent O'Brien, the daddy of all dual-purpose trainers, and with whom Michael had spent a spell learning his trade.

After proving himself a great trainer of jumpers, Michael might well have hit the heights on the flat...given one or two like Rodrigo De Triano and Dr Devious!

My reaction to the news that Shergar would run in the St Leger was... THIS IS ONE TO BET AGAINST! Easier thought than done, because although the Leger line-up was only seven-strong, the classic looked tricky. Obviously, the supporters of Shergar thought the issue was cut-and-dried. For my money, Shergar was never going to stay the Doncaster distance. He was too speedy - certainly one of the fastest Derby winners I have ever seen. And it has been my experience that fast horses don't stay. I went for a one-two Leger bet on Glint of Gold, who proceeded to finish well ahead of Shergar, but had to settle for second best behind Dick Hern's out-and-out stayer, Cut Above.

It was also in second spot that Laurel Queen laboured home behind Hickory Wind when starting 5-1 on for Carlisle's Levy Board Apprentice Stakes.

If Laurel Queen ever had an off-day, that was it! Opposed by only Hickory Wind, Ayodessa and Stradbroke, victory for Laurel Queen (a seven lengths winner of her previous race, at

Hamilton), was generally regarded as a formality. Laurel Queen didn't see eye to eye with that view. She started to become restless in the parade ring, where Stradbroke was being led around on a long rein. This worried Jack, who remarked: "I'm wondering whether that one is going to be troublesome at the start. I hope nothing happens to upset Laurel Queen."

There was an upset...and it occurred just as the horses left the parade ring. Rearing up until she was beyond the point of no return, and with her young rider, Wally Hollick, unable to do anything about it, Laurel Queen turned right over and landed on her back, legs threshing the air. First fears were obviously that she might have injured herself. Back on an even keel, she seemed all right, and Jack was satisfied that no damage was done. Wally hopped back on board, and took her down to the start without further problems.

The Carlisle going was officially termed "hard". Probably "concrete" would be a more apt description of the Cumbria course's fast terrain, which has been referred to by jockeys as "an extension of the M6."

On this occasion, the course was both hard and rough. Laurel Queen looked as happy on it as a cat on a hot tin roof. As she chased Hickory Wind around the bottom turn, and up the straight, we waited in vain for her to master the leader. For those who had bet the odds-on, it was a case of gone with the "Wind," as the leader kept up the gallop to beat the ill-at-ease Laurel Queen by two and a half lengths. It was a sad outcome for Wally Hollick. Still seeking his first winner, after many placed rides, Jack's apprentice must have been dreaming that his big day had arrived.

33

On many another day, Laurel Queen would have taken such a modest contest by the scruff of the neck and shown Wally the way to the winner's enclosure.  We could only assume that Laurel Queen's unsettling pre-race experience contributed to the reverse.

Thankfully, there was no lasting mark.  She returned to win three more times that season, giving her a 1991 score of six, and taking her career tally to nine.  When the Laurel horse, Surrey Dancer, was a beaten 7-1 on chance, at Cartmel, in May 1994, Jack Berry asked me the following day: "Have you got over it?"

"I still haven't got over that shock with Laurel Queen at Carlisle," I replied.  Jack admitted that he still thought about it from time to time.

Immediately after the Carlisle event, I recall a member of the racing press approaching Jack and asking him to comment about the shock defeat: "Well," Jack replied, with the assured-ness of a battle scarred veteran of a variety of testing Turf situations, "I'm not going to pack up training."

# CHAPTER 6

## KING OF CLUBS

Don White has something in common with Tommy Docherty in that he's had more clubs than Jack Nicklaus. Rarely has a week gone by in recent years without Don White leading in a winner. They call him "King of Clubs." He's a member of Laurel Racing Club, but keeps his other memberships up his sleeve, like aces. He played one of these aces, much to the surprise of some of his racing acquaintances, at a Beverley meeting. Many photographs of Laurel Queen feature Don in a starring role...leading in the winner! But when Don was seen leading in Sunday Mail Lass following a Beverley success, some racegoers thought that he might be out of order. Sunday Mail Lass, trained by Jack Berry, runs for the Scottish Sunday Mail Racing Club. "Surely, you're not a member of that Club?" queried a punter, obviously thinking that the Scottish outfit was a bit off Don's beaten track. "Oh yes, I'm a member," Don proudly asserted as he did the leading-in honours with Sunday Mail Lass. He explained: "Jack Berry visualised that there could be a day when Sunday Mail Lass won away from a Scottish course, and there might not be many Club members present. He suggested that I join the Club, then there would always be someone to lead in their horses. It's all worked out according to plan." Whether Don will have bought a photograph, as a memento of the occasion is doubtful. It would cost him a packet to keep pace with the "clicks" of racecourse photographers.

One photographer threatened to down tools when he saw Don

standing alongside a Wetherby winner.  That was after our dual purpose performer, Majed, trained by Mary Reveley, had won a Wetherby handicap hurdle.  Fortunately, the proposed industrial action by racecourse photographer, Colin Turner, came to an amicable conclusion.

The turf needs its ardent on-course supporters like Don White, who is regularly seen at the races with his wife and son.  He takes all the banter with a great sense of humour, commenting: "It's all good fun," adding with a hearty laugh: "I've had more winners than Sheikh Mohammed."

For Don and the rest of us, however, the shock defeat of Laurel Queen at Carlisle marked the start of a mid-season drought as far as her contributions were concerned.  There were compensations for the Laurel Club as Laurel Queen's efforts dried up. We had acquired Rose Glen after a claimer at Haydock.  We did a deal with owner, David Furlong, so that we could lease the mare until the end of the season.  Our association with the horse turned out to be much more brief than that but it was "Roses" all the way.

On the July Saturday that Rose Glen was making her debut in our colours at Ayr, we also had Laurel Queen in a mile handicap at a Southwell all-weather meeting.

Rose Glen had remained with Alan Bailey - then based at Newmarket - following the Haydock win.

The ambitious game plan was now to go for an Ayr double with Rose Glen in Saturday and Monday events.  All went well in the first leg, with Sharon Murgatroyd confidently bringing Rose Glen home a length clear of Melancolia in the Scots Wha'hae Amateur Handicap.  Sadly, this was to be the last winning ride before Sharon's amateur career was tragically ended by a jumping fall.

Pat and I stayed up at Ayr over the weekend for Rose Glen's Monday race. There was no joy for us from Laurel Queen's Saturday evening outing at Southwell. She was well down the field, and this was her second failure since the Carlisle apprentice race flop. A return to Carlisle when starting favourite for a claimer had seen her lead three furlongs out then fade into fifth place behind the 25-1 chance, Annaceramic.

On the Monday of our Ayr weekend we found ourselves once again back in the cauldron of the claiming race scene. Rose Glen duly completed the double in the hands of Andrew Tucker, winning a shade cleverly from Light Hand. The claiming aspect was left to "pot luck," and that turned out to be a big mistake. A claim was put in for Rose Glen by Tony Collins, of Gay Future "Cartmel coup" fame. Alan Bailey tried to persuade him to "take a profit," but Tony Collins was determined to hang on to the horse. Pat and I headed home... with Alan Bailey and David Furlong still attempting to make the "new owner" change his mind. The outcome was that Alan continued to train Rose Glen and that David was able to buy the mare back at the end of the season. For the Laurel Club it was a short but sweet relationship with Rose Glen, two runs, two wins. She was subsequently to cross swords with Laurel Queen. But on arriving home we found that our heroine had been put on the sidelines for a while.

I rang the stables and Jo Berry told me that Laurel Queen was "a bit stiff behind" following the race at Southwell. It was hoped that a rest for two or three weeks would put her right. Just over a month later, she was ready for a return to action at Newcastle. Jack reported that Laurel Queen was going well at home, but that she might just be a shade short of her best after the lay-off. Over the mile of Newcastle's Gallowgate Claimer, Laurel Queen was soon dictating the pace in a 13-strong field, but I couldn't see her keeping it up. It was only inside the final furlong that she relinquished the lead as her old rival, Stairway To Heaven, produced a strong run to win by two lengths from Golden Chip. Laurel Queen faded into fifth spot, but she was less than three lengths behind the winner, and I was delighted by this comeback. John Carroll said she would come on for the run, and Jack Berry was also well pleased. Stairway To Heaven had previously recaptured winning form when equipped with blinkers.

She again wore "the blinds" and we regarded the Newcastle form as a reliable yardstick to Laurel Queen being nearly back at her best. I now had visions of Don White leading her in next time out. As it was some time since her last win (Hamilton, in May) we felt confident that we could run Laurel Queen in another claimer without much fear of losing her. I had told our club members not to back her at Newcastle. But she now appeared primed as a punting proposition in claiming company. The City Cab Fillies' Claiming Stakes, over a mile at Edinburgh, on September 16, seemed a likely event for putting Laurel Queen back on the road to success. That's all things being equal. But are they ever in racing? It's said that on the turf and under it, all MEN are equal. But sometimes a LADY can have fearsome odds to overcome. Laurel Queen was certainly to have the odds stacked against her at Edinburgh.

# CHAPTER 7

## THE DAY THAT RAIN CAME DOWN

We have been known to have good luck at declaration time when eagerly waiting to see what Laurel Queen would be up against. When the declarations came through for the Edinburgh event we had to view the situation with mixed feelings. While the opposition wasn't strong enough to have John Carroll quaking in his riding boots, a field of 14 could cause him some problems. We had not expected so many declarations, and adding to our worries was a No. 2 draw. In a mile race at Edinburgh there can be something of a cavalry charge to the sharp right-hand bend. It was difficult to visualise Laurel Queen being able to make all the running from her outside berth. John would just have to ride according to the way things went from the off. But the troubles had only just begun.

The weather, as the Monday meeting got under way, was ideal for washing day...bright and breezy. Laurel Queen's race was the fourth on the card. By that time the wind had picked up somewhat, but the sun was still shining.

The main topic of conversation in the parade ring was Laurel Queen's difficult draw position. "It isn't essential that she makes the running, so John will just have to bide his time if she fails to get a fast start," said Jack Berry. Despite the draw, there was no doubt that Laurel Queen was worth a bet. But there was further cause for reconsideration about punting possibilities when the weather suddenly underwent a dramatic change. The wind was bringing dark clouds rolling over, and suddenly big spots of rain pattered upon us. Within a matter of seconds, the spots turned to stair rods, and there was an ultra-rapid exit from the parade ring by all except the jockeys and horses, and a few unfortunate trainers who hadn't completed their tasks. It was an instant monsoon, accompanied by murk, and I was wet through in galloping less than 50 yards to get under cover. Still needing to get a bet on, I dashed another 20 yards across open ground to Ladbrokes' shop. By this time, my suit was absolutely soaked, with another dousing to come as I decided to run across to the weighing room.

Jack and secretary Pat had also made their way to the weighing room to watch the race on the closed circuit TV. That was the intention - but there was precious little to see. The torrential rain and mist made us wonder if the race might be subject to a lengthy delay. Eventually we could see "ghostly" figures being loaded into the stalls. From the "off" it was just possible to discern that Laurel Queen was slowly away. Then the runners became just a bunch of shadowy shapes heading for the top turn. The picture became slightly clearer rounding the bend, and for a moment I glimpsed Laurel Queen on the outside, and she seemed to be making up some ground. In the home straight, we were in much the same boat as the race commentator...waiting for the leaders to gallop out of the rain and gloom. What a tremendous thrill when I saw Laurel Queen coming up the outside with a storming run. The horses were racing directly into the wind. And as Laurel Queen disputed the lead with Sharp Money just inside the final furlong, the duo momentarily lost their action as they were hit by a gale force gust.

Laurel Queen looked as if she was shrugging it off as "all in the day's work" as she got back on an even keel for John to bring her home three lengths ahead of Sharp Money. How that weighing room echoed to our urgings in the final furlong! It was one of the most epic, and dramatic races I have "never" seen. Secretary Pat was as "over the moon" as any football manager, and gave Jack a big hug.

After Laurel Queen's battle against the elements, she had to endure the gauntlet of congratulatory pats and slaps from our ecstatic club members. For John and the other jockeys involved, it was a somewhat squelchy return to the weighing room. They were so saturated, with boots full of water, that they weighed-in 4lbs heavier! John said: "I think it worked out for the best that she was slowly away. A horse wouldn't want to be out in front for too long in conditions like that. We gradually made up ground, and she was strong at the finish when the leaders were coming back to us." We treasure a video of that race. At least we can see the part that matters. Amazingly as the runners cross the line, the visibility is becoming good, just as quickly as it went bad.

Jack said that Laurel Queen had an advantage because "it was typical Cockerham weather." As if to prove the point, he declared Laurel Queen for a seven furlongs event at Southwell only four days later. I had been under the impression that Laurel Queen would give Southwell a miss after her trip to Scotland and exertions in bad weather. Therefore it was a shock - if you'll pardon the pun - to see her in the line-up of 14 for the East Midlands Electricity Claiming Stakes.

At Edinburgh, Laurel Queen had started at the fair price of 4-1, joint favourite with Sharp Money. The Southwell opposition looked stronger, with Unanimous and Restore well-fancied. Laurel Queen seemed to have reasonable each-way prospects, provided she was none the worse for the Musselburgh mission. John Carroll was unable to do the weight of 7st 13lb. So the mount went to capable lightweight, Nicky Carlisle. Talk about tricky for Nicky! He needed to get in and out of more pockets than Fagan to land the spoils.

Drawn No.2 on the inside, Laurel Queen didn't get the best of breaks, and her partner was looking for room throughout the race. Every time that Nicky asked Laurel Queen to go through a gap, she responded without hesitation. The filly looked as though she was enjoying a game of hide and seek. She weaved through until asked to challenge in between Unanimous and African Chimes at the furlong marker. Producing superior speed, Laurel Queen sprinted through the narrow gap to forge two lengths clear of Unanimous. After keeping us on tenter-hooks for most of the contest, Laurel Queen finally won in comfortable style. Support for 6-4 favourite Unanimous - out to follow-up a well-backed Leicester success - enabled Laurel Queen to land a 5-1 touch, which was very nice indeed, with our pockets already well-lined from Edinburgh. Jack was a good judge, running her so soon after Edinburgh. Mary Reveley, who watched the race on SIS, said: "She's a game filly to go through gaps like that." This was Laurel Queen's fifth win of the season, and put her one behind the Channel 4 Trophy leaders, her stablemates, Paris House and Doublova.

An engagement had been made for Laurel Queen in a mile claimer at Nottingham. This came only three days after the Southwell success. With Laurel Queen winning so easily, Jack said: "I'll see how she is on Sunday morning. She's so well at the moment, we could run her again." Sure enough, Jack declared her in an attempt to complete a hat-trick within the space of eight days. Some critics have said that our filly was found a succession of soft options to win so many races, and that claiming events provided easy pickings. Such opinion amounted to being wise after the event. If these races were so easy to win, why did Laurel Queen start at 4-1 and then 5-1 at Edinburgh and Southwell? And why was she a 7-1 chance in the betting on Nottingham's Carlton Claiming Stakes? These races were very competitive - plenty of runners, and several with a chance. In a Nottingham field of 20, the betting market was headed by Lord Oberon and Tea Dust, at 3-1. Once again, we fancied Laurel Queen as an each-way proposition.

Gary Carter was renewing acquaintance with her, and was optimistic about her chance. We would have to trust to luck that Laurel Queen got a clear run from her No. 19 draw. A low draw might have seemed more promising, but nothing could be guaranteed in such a big field. Laurel Queen was one of the first into the stalls - which turned out to be a blow to our chances. The rest of them took a long time to load. And after standing there as good as gold for what seemed like an age, restlessness took over at the split second the stalls sprung open. Rearing up, Laurel Queen nearly put Gary on the floor. By the time she was in her stride, all hat-trick hope was lost. Gary could do no more than go through the motions, and allow Laurel Queen to come home in her own good time, as Lester Piggott and Lord Oberon took the prize from Tea Dust and Willie Carson. Obviously, plenty of Nottingham punters were not complaining.

We felt that we must have gone close to winning but for losing so much ground at the start. Gary confirmed that, saying: "I couldn't believe how well she was behaving in the stalls. Then she reared just as they opened." Laurel Queen had run on to finish about eight lengths adrift of the winner, and at least we knew she was retaining her form at this late-September stage. I didn't think that a friendly claim would be required. I did consider claiming the winner, and while still pondering over the possibility, I went to the weighing room to pick up a claim form. The clerk of the scales gave me the form, and then as I turned away, I was confronted by the winner's trainer, Ben Hanbury. "Are you putting in a claim? I just want to know so that I might be able to save the owners some money." I thought that the way Hanbury approached me was rude. And that he was naive in expecting me to tell him if I was claiming his horse.

I considered putting in a claim of £12,000 for Lord Oberon, then decided against it. That turned out to be a mistake. Lord Oberon was later to bring more than double that price at the autumn sales. And after Nottingham, he won a Newcastle handicap worth £3,850. The man who never made a mistake must not have attempted anything approaching ambition. I was to make another mistake in respect of Laurel Queen's next race, at Wolverhampton, where John Carroll and Jack Berry also shared in "carrying the can."

# CHAPTER 8

## TWO TOO MANY

Ask punters what they think of trainers saddling two or more runners in a race, and the consensus will be that they don't like it. If the trainer wins with the outsider the common cry is: "It's a twist." Traditionally trainers have used this means to confuse punters as to what they were up to. Several years ago, I was privy to some information regarding a Catterick two-year-old event in which a northern trainer had dual involvement. An "unfashionable" jockey was on the fancied one. An owner connected with the stable told me: "This horse has so much in hand that the jockey will have to fall off to lose." The horse was freely offered at 10-1... until the signal given for the Catterick coup to commence. All prices were taken, until wiped off the boards completely, leaving late participants in this huge punt to scramble to the Tote windows as a last resort. Did it win? As sure as the Tatts bookmaker laid me 10-1, it hacked up. Nice work if you're on the inside.

Nowadays, owners and trainers are often dually represented in races for no other reason than the necessity of giving horses an outing. Sheikh Mohammed has a lot of horses and the trainers have to run them somewhere. It's the same with Jack Berry and his two-year-olds. Also with his older sprinters. They often clash, running strictly on their merits. Jack will be happy with any winner, whatever the betting market says about respective chances. Running two is not always a good idea. We had Laurel Delight (Frankie Dettori) running against Press The Bell (John Carroll) in a 1993 sprint event at

Chester. Jack told me that John wanted to be on Press The
Bell because when Gary Carter won on the latter in his previous race at Lingfield he said: "I've never been as fast in my
life!" In the Chester sprint, Laurel Delight went a bit faster
than Press The Bell, but the pace-making tussle meant that
they cut each other's throat, leaving opponents to come from
way behind and overhaul them in the short straight. Jack
Berry wasn't pleased. Neither was I, but such a happening
could have been anticipated.

When Laurel Queen, refreshed by a break of just over three
weeks following her starting "stall" at Nottingham, contested a
mid-October claimer at Wolverhampton, I gave Jack the go-
ahead to run Kestrel Forboxes as well. Although a better two-
year-old than Laurel Queen - winning a maiden event at Bath,
a £10,000 seller at York, and a nursery at Windsor - Kestrel
Forboxes had not made the anticipated progress in his second
campaign. We had managed to place him to win three times in
claimers at Carlisle, Catterick and Haydock, but had decided
to let him go to the autumn sales. The Wolverhampton ground,
although officially "good," had some soft patches. We didn't
regard the conditions as ideal, but I fully expected Laurel
Queen to finish ahead of Kestrel Forboxes and to be "there-
abouts" at the finish. The outcome was to leave me kicking
myself for allowing both Laurel Queen and Kestrel Forboxes to
run.

In a field of 16, the betting market was headed by Just A Step,
who was returning after a three months' absence. Maybe the
bookies were remembering how Mat McCormack had sent out
Just A Step to beat Tea Dust and land a gamble at Goodwood
in June. Laurel Queen started at 15-2 (regarded as great each-
way value) with Kestrel Forboxes a 12-1 chance.

46

Gary Carter rode Kestrel Forboxes and made the running for five furlongs. John Carroll seemed all too anxious to keep tabs on the leader. He had Laurel Queen in front over two furlongs out, and although looking all over a winner, along came Darren Biggs and Brown Fairy to hit the front in the last 100 yards. The inquest verdict had to be that running Kestrel Forboxes cost Laurel Queen the race. "She should have won. We have to blame John for that," said Jack. I thought that another contributory factor to the reverse was that Brown Fairy had raced on better ground towards the outside in the home straight. Unable to attend the meeting, I watched the race on SIS in a Ladbrokes shop. A "regular" told me that no horse had won racing on the far side from four events that afternoon.

I dashed off to get in telephone contact with secretary Pat, who was at Wolverhampton to keep an eye on the claiming race proceedings. I instructed her: "If any claim goes in, make a friendly claim for Laurel Queen. We'll take our chance with Kestrel Forboxes because he's going to the sales." A claim was tendered and Pat duly did her duty on behalf of Laurel Queen. However, the rival claim turned out to be for Kestrel Forboxes. He was claimed for £5,250. Since then, he has raced with success in Jersey. Viewing the Wolverhampton race on video at a later date, John conceded to Jack: "It was my fault. I should have won that one, boss."

Laurel Queen was retaining her form remarkably well as we neared the end of October, having been on the go since her Warwick seasonal debut win on April 2nd. The enforced break when returning home stiff behind following her July run at Southwell, must have helped to keep her going.

It was yet another competitive claimer in which Laurel Queen lined up at Leicester. With Gary Carter back on board in a field of 19 for the mile Fosse Way Claiming Stakes, Laurel Queen was 4-1 joint favourite along with the Pat Eddery-part-nered Midnight Saga. Our filly had not been seen to front-run-ning effect for some time, and this contest over Leicester's searching straight mile didn't inspire the revival of such tac-tics. So the game plan was that Gary would ride a waiting race. I respected the chance of Tohamah, saddled by Henry Cecil. I presumed that Cecil was present primarily to saddle hot favourite Pabouche, a winner for him earlier in the after-noon. Drawn 17, towards the far side, Laurel Queen had plen-ty of rivals ahead of her at the half-way stage. Then Gary gradually started to make up ground until in a challenging position before the final furlong. Laurel Queen surged clear for a three lengths victory over Genuine Lady, with Tohamah third. Gary reported: "She did it really well and took me to the front a shade sooner than expected but she had plenty left in the last furlong."

What a tremendous servant Laurel Queen was proving to be. With six wins to her credit, she remained in the Channel 4 Trophy running along with stablemates, Paris House and Doublova. But we came very close to losing her in an unguard-ed moment during the Leicester "claiming time."

I had made out a friendly claim form, and waited in the weigh-ing room to see if any claims were tendered. Fortunately, sec-retary Pat was also keeping an eye on things for Laurel Queen had no greater fan. It had seemed that we would get away with another no claims bonus. But as the final minutes ticked away, and while I was talking to someone, Pat said: "Quick...a claim has gone in." I instantly put my friendly claim in the tray. To my astonishment, the man who had tendered the rival claim, pulled out a stop-watch and said to the clerk of the scales: "That claim is too late." If ever there was a "frivolous" objection, this was it. He should have known better than to try and dictate to a racecourse official like the clerk of the scales. I thought the official was going to burst a blood vessel.

"I'll be the one deciding when the claiming time is up, and there's a minute to go yet," he snapped. He must have been pleased when our friendly claim won the day. Pat breathed a sigh of relief. "Imagine if that man had got his hands on Laurel Queen. It doesn't stand thinking about." I believe "that man" had wanted Laurel Queen for racing somewhere on the Continent. With that bid thwarted, we now turned our attention to looking for one last throw of the dice with Laurel Queen in an attempt to clinch the Channel 4 Trophy. The season had less than two weeks remaining, so suitable opportunities were few. No more claimers, but that pleased secretary Pat following the Leicester anxieties.

A mile handicap at Edinburgh gave us our last chance, but with Laurel Queen penalised 5lb for the Leicester win, and the ground softening up, we viewed this excursion with hope rather than confidence. The Edinburgh card opened with a claimer, but it was over a distance of one mile, three furlongs, 32 yards. Too far for our horse. Not that a claimer over the more ideal trip of seven furlongs or a mile would have been any use on the day. As a three-year-old, Laurel Queen didn't like soft ground. Despite all the rain when she won at Edinburgh, the ground had remained good. In the claiming race, there was a popular outcome with 6-4 favourite Dizzy winning easily. I thought of claiming Dizzy - then trained by Barry Hills - for hurdling, but doubted if she had the physique for the jumping game. Dizzy did go on to make a very good hurdler for the Peter Montieth stable.

After seeing them plough through the mud in the claimer, I

was even less optimistic about Laurel Queen's chance in the handicap, which was the fourth event on the card. In a field of 15, Laurel Queen was drawn on the outside. Her starting price of 10-1 summed up her prospects. Never in the hunt, she came home a bogged-down tenth behind Languedoc, with Ashdren and Namaste placed. "She was never going on that ground," John Carroll reported.

The Channel 4 Trophy had a luckless outcome for Jack Berry, with Laurel Queen, Paris House and Doublova ending the season on the six mark, but with victory going to Peter Savill's Sense of Priority (trained by Peter Easterby) by virtue of a superior record of placed runs.

You can't win them all, and as Jack asserted: "Laurel Queen has done us proud. She'll be back to win more races for us next season. Maybe the handicapper will drop us a couple of pounds for her defeat at Edinburgh."

# CHAPTER 9

## NO TO JUMPING

Towards the end of Laurel Queen's three-year-old career, we had considered sending her to Mary Reveley to see if she would make a hurdler. Initially, Mary was interested, then she wondered if the filly had been given too busy a time on the flat. Then Jack said: "If you want to try her over hurdles, I'll train her." But after further consideration, I told Jack: "We'll forget about the jumping. She's won nine times in two seasons. What more could we ask? Put her away until next season." The decision delighted Jack.

The 1992 flat season opened with a surprise. Jack had to wait until the second day for his first winner! He seemed a shade stunned that the odds-on Sabre Ratfler could finish only third in the Brocklesby.

Another of his two-year-olds, Classic Storm, although blind in her left eye, knew where the winning post was in the Doncaster seller. The Berry bandwagon was rolling, and Fylde Flyer, cheered on by members of the West Lancashire Gazette owners' group, notched an 8-1 win in the following day's Cammidge Trophy.

Later in March, Laurel Queen was back in action...on the Beverley beat. Our four-year-old had wintered really well. "She's been going nicely in home work and should take a bit of beating at Beverley," Jack reported. The Withernsea Handicap was very competitive and Laurel Queen was a 10-1 chance in a line-up of 14. I have given up betting each way with the racecourse bookmakers. The way they "shade" the odds if offering the each-way facility is diabolical. For instance, Laurel Queen would be 10-1 with bookmakers betting win only but around 7-1 with those taking each-way bets. I would rather pay the on-course tax of 6 per cent and bet each-way at the racecourse betting shop.

I had been anxious about the Beverley ground conditions - reported to be on the soft side a few days before the race. The weather forecast gave us some hope, and the going turned out to be perfect. In races staged over the extended seven furlongs, and one mile plus, at Beverley, I would prefer a horse to be drawn towards the inside, although there is no guarantee of a clear run. After the downhill run on the far side, trouble can be encountered on the bend and when there is "bunching" on the uphill run for home. I can recall more horses running into difficulties at Beverley than on any other course. Laurel Queen was to prove no exception to the rule. There's one way to get a clear run - make all the running! That's what Michael Roberts proceeded to do on the Clive Brittain-trained Colossus. This didn't surprise us, because Colossus had won a Haydock handicap in this style on his final start in 1991. While Colossus was nipping around Beverley's bottom-bend and heading for home, Laurel Queen was in the mid-division and looking short of room. It was only approaching the final furlong that John Carroll was able to show Laurel Queen some daylight. Finishing with a flourish, Laurel Queen was cutting down the leader's advantage, but Colossus was able to prevail by a length and a half. The comment in my form book was that Laurel Queen "would have gone close with a clear run."

We had to be happy enough about Laurel Queen's seasonal debut display in such a competitive handicap. Jack was justifiably pleased with the run, commenting: "It was a very nice start. She'll come on for the run, and we'll find another handicap for her."

A return to Beverley was to prove luckier. But before that, Laurel Queen was to suffer a Hamilton reverse that would prove favourable to us in the long-term. The Standard Life Handicap, staged over Hamilton's extended mile, was nominated for our filly's second outing of the season. Whereas our weather worries had proved groundless at Beverley, Laurel Queen was to become a Hamilton stick-in-the-mud. The going was officially described as good to soft (soft in places). I visualised this Scottish venture having a similar outcome to her 1991 finale at Edinburgh.

It was not generally accepted among the punting fraternity that Laurel Queen required good or fast ground to be seen at her best. Later in her career, she didn't seem to mind the mud. But at this stage, she couldn't cope with it. Nevertheless, punters seemed prepared to judge her Hamilton chance on promising Beverley form. The seven opponents included our dual winner of the previous season Rose Glen, now back in the colours of David Furlong, and still trained by Alan Bailey. You can tell when people fancy their horses. It must be years of involvement giving you the instinct. I didn't need to ask David and Alan if they fancied Rose Glen. It was written all over them in the parade ring. Jack was trying to induce some optimism into us about Laurel Queen's prospects. But I was convinced that the April showers - the kind that last for hours - had sunk Laurel Queen's chance. It was more by way of curiosity than any intention to back her that I went to look at her odds with the bookmakers. She was 5-2 favourite, but I wouldn't have had a shirt button on at 10-1. Of course, I could have been proved wrong. I was hoping I was wrong. But Laurel

Queen ran very much in line with my expectations.

The early running was made by Mofador, then Blue Grit led until the distance. Gary Carter attempted to improve Laurel Queen's position from the rear of the field, but she was not travelling at all well on the ground. Rose Glen made some headway, but the one leaving them all standing in the final furlong was Majed, ridden by the claimer Jason Weaver. Absolutely sluicing through the mud, Majed took over from Blue Grit and then surged well clear. Rose Glen beat Blue Grit for second, with Laurel Queen floundering into fourth spot. It was a most impressive success by Majed, who had been upped to this handicap company following a clear-cut mudlarking victory in a Folkestone claimer. Majed was a 5-1 chance. With hindsight, what a wonderful price that was. This scintillating win by Majed was now well and truly etched on my mind. Racing on "good to firm" ground at Newmarket less than a week later, Majed was not the same force, although running reasonably well to finish fourth behind Myfontaine in a handicap field of 13.

Nine days later, Majed figured among the opposition to Laurel Queen in a Beverley claimer staged over one mile, 100 yards. Those 100 yards worried me. It was the longest distance tackled by Laurel Queen, although her previous season's success at Hamilton gave us some encouragement. Strictly on her latest running at Hamilton, Laurel Queen could hardly be fancied to cope with Majed. But this was an entirely different ball game. The going was now good, and in our favour, whereas Majed was a tried and tested mudlarking type. Plus we had a favourable No. 13 draw in a field of 16, while Majed was drawn No. 1 on the outside. There was no way that Majed could jump and go in the style of Laurel Queen's previous Beverley conqueror, Colossus. He would have to do it the hard way - coming from behind. And he was 4lb worse off. Betting was tight between the two, with Majed 2-1 favourite and Laurel Queen 5-2. There was no specific instruction given to John Carroll, but we felt that he needed to keep something in the tank for those last uphill 100 yards. If we were unlucky on our previous visit to Beverley, everything was to go unbelievably well this time.

As Jo Fanning blazed the trail on Magdalene, John was able to tuck Laurel Queen away on the inside and concentrate on obtaining a clear passage on the bend. Laurel Queen had a dream of a run and raced up the straight in Magdalene's slipstream, before John moved her to the leader's outside.
John was now sitting in the driving seat, waiting to press the accellerator and get first run. Laurel Queen was easing herself into the lead two furlongs out as Magdalene dropped away. John said go and stole a march as Yonge Tender and Majed (coming from well back) produced strong, late efforts. The trio flashed past the post with little between them, although we were confident that Laurel Queen had won.

I anticipated a three-horse photo finish, but the judged called Laurel Queen first, and a photo for second. Nevertheless, the distances were a short head, and the same. I was delighted with Laurel Queen's display as she would have won comfortably at the mile distance.
And the turn-around of form with Majed - a difference of about nine lengths - demonstrated the importance of ground conditions. Everything continued to go in our favour...there was no claim for Laurel Queen. Later on the card, there was a boost to Laurel Queen's credentials when Colossus took a handicap under 9st 10lb. That didn't stop us from looking for another claiming event for Laurel Queen's follow-up bid.

# CHAPTER 10

## CARLISLE UPS AND DOWNS

The mixed fortunes experienced by Laurel Queen in her Carlisle excursions continued when she returned to the Cumbria course to contest a mile claimer. The April showers had either continued into early May, or the rain was telling us that summer was here, at last!

The Buttermere claimer was staged in two divisions. Laurel Queen was in the first division, but I felt that the rain meant "relegation." She was very easy in the betting market at 4-1. I would have wanted to snap up half that price with the going in Laurel Queen's favour. I kept my cash in my pocket. As she was carrying 7st 11lb, and John Carroll could only do 8st 2lb, we booked lightweight Lindsay Charnock to ride. In a field of 10, Laurel Queen was struggling from the start on ground officially described as "good to soft" ("soft in places"). The ground did, indeed, look very patchy. Happy enough in the mud, however, proved to be the 3-1 favourite, Just A Step, whom Billy Newnes steered to an all-the-way victory. Laurel Queen, continually ill-at-ease in her action, lost fourth place in a photo finish with Kagram Queen, but she was over six lengths behind the winner. On this occasion, there was no need to hold an inquest into "what went wrong." By now, I felt that my opinion regarding Laurel Queen's dislike of soft ground had been clearly vindicated. In future, I would be more determined to steer her away from competing in such conditions. At least, there was nothing in Laurel Queen's running to encourage anyone to put in a claim for her.

# LAUREL QUEEN

Whether Laurel Queen's unhappy experience at Redcar as a two-year-old was remembered by her in a couple of subsequent visits there, would be impossible to say. But if she was still racing today, and we ran her at either Redcar or Pontefract, I wouldn't want to back her.

There was no complaint about the ground conditions when Laurel Queen went on from Carlisle to compete in a seven furlongs Redcar claimer. As in her outing at the Cleveland course as a juvenile - when incurring an eye injury - she was drawn on the outside of the field. Stall No. 1 in a 12-horse line-up didn't encourage many punters to give her a chance. Apart from the difficulty presented by the draw, the opposition included a couple - Ringland and Finjan - meeting our horse on much more favourable terms than would have applied in a handicap. The well-weighted duo proceeded to dominate this claimer to justify their betting market position of 2-1 joint favourites. Just to show that punters can be good judges, there was only a short-head between them as Ringland snatched the spoils. A very fast early pace set by Sammy Slew soon had Laurel Queen in trouble. John Carroll said ; "Obviously she was seeing plenty of daylight towards the outside, and she was run off her feet early on. I thought there was no point being hard on her when her chance had gone. She didn't seem at her best today." The fact that Laurel Queen started a 16-1 chance emphasised that she had faced a tough task. This was an instance of how a claimer can be more difficult to win than a handicap. Laurel Queen finished ninth of the 12 runners. I felt that she was really better than that.

On returning home, Jack found that she was "a bit stiff." Consequently, he gave her an easy time for a week or so. And although given the go-ahead for a return to Carlisle just over three weeks after the Redcar run, we felt that she might be a shade short of concert pitch.

The event chosen was the Cumbria Fillies' Claimer, over seven furlongs. The going was "hard." In a field of seven, the newspaper tipsters plumped for Greetland Folly as a "good thing." According to the official handicap ratings, she had pounds in hand of all the opposition. I wasn't so sure that Greetland Folly was at her best, even though she had finished third in a Doncaster fillies' handicap when shouldering 9st 7lb. Neither could I be sure that Laurel Queen was spot-on after her brief break. But weighing up all the fitness factors, etc., Laurel Queen had to be worth a bet at 6-1. Greetland Folly was always odds-on and started at 4-7. I plumped for a one-two bet on Laurel Queen. I felt that she would either win or finish second to the favourite.

Ravecino set the pace until John Carroll sent Laurel Queen on about 2½ furlongs out. At this stage, Tony Culhane was clearly finding Greetland Folly going like anything but a "good thing." A challenger to Laurel Queen did emerge in the final furlong. But it was the second favourite, Tommy Fairhurst's Spanish Performer, coming out of the pack under Jo Fanning's guidance to stretch Laurel Queen. Although Laurel Queen's lead was diminishing, she managed to hold off Spanish Performer by a head, with the third-placed Ravecino eight lengths away, and Greetland Folly only fourth. There's nothing like winning....any kind of race, whatever the starting price. But odds of 6-1 certainly put some nice icing on the cake! John told us that Laurel Queen had "blown up." He added: "It was only her guts keeping her going in the last furlong. She'll be all the better for the race." Jack agreed that the run would have brought Laurel Queen back to her best following her enforced short break early in June.

Armed with this knowledge, we were confident that Laurel Queen could win another claimer at Edinburgh just over a fortnight later. Spanish Performer again figured in the opposition, but we felt sure that Laurel Queen's Carlisle superiority would now be more marked. Many of the newspaper tipsters did nominate one to beat us in the mile Dunbar Claiming Stakes. They thought that Inseyab, trained by Patrick Haslam, was the one to be on. Drawn No. 7 of the eight contestants, John Carroll had Laurel Queen off to a flyer from this favourable pitch. Edinburgh's bottom bend can be tricky to negotiate. After the right-hand turn, some horses lose ground by moving wide. But Laurel Queen always seemed happy enough racing around this bend, whether on the inside or outside. John experienced no problems keeping her on an even keel, and she was round the turn and heading for home in great style. A hot pursuer was Mbulwa, with Inseyab making headway after getting off to a sluggish start. Mbulwa maintained a persistent challenge for Jimmy Fortune, but John was always looking like he had something in hand, and brought Laurel Queen home a half-length ahead. Mbulwa was two lengths clear of Inseyab. It was the 13th of July, but for us it was the 12th win of Laurel Queen's career. I wasn't alone in keeping an anxious eye on the Edinburgh claiming race tray. The respective connections of Mbulwa and Inseyab were also keen to keep their horse. It was a happy conclusion for all concerned.

# CHAPTER 11

## SCOTTISH CHEERS FOR QUEEN

Five days after our successful Edinburgh excursion, we were back on the Scottish trail... this time with Laurel Queen's target a seven furlongs claimer at Ayr. I don't know whether Patrick Haslam thought that we might not return to Scotland so soon with Laurel Queen, but he declared Inseyab at the overnight stage. We were pleased to find only four remaining in the race. I couldn't see Princess Maxine, running on her home course for Linda Perratt's stable, beating us. Valley of Time would be the outsider of the party. So the Campbeltown Claiming Stakes seemed to be all about whether Laurel Queen could confirm Edinburgh superiority over Inseyab, who was 2lb better off. Laurel Queen edged favouritism at 6-4, with Inseyab 13-8, Princess Maxine 5-2 and Valley of Time 14-1. We felt fully entitled to fancy our chance of winning again.

Laurel Queen had made the anticipated improvement in between Carlisle and Edinburgh, and we thought that she was now really at her best.

There was an anxious moment when Laurel Queen reared as the stalls opened, but she didn't lose a lot of ground. This served to settle the riding tactics for John Carroll, who could now forget any thoughts of winning in all-the-way Edinburgh style. Princess Maxine set the pace until approaching the seventh and final furlong where John pushed Laurel Queen ahead. Kevin Darley and Inseyab were persistent challengers in the closing stages, but John kept Laurel Queen going to win by a head. Taking into account the weights, the first two ran very much in line with Edinburgh form.

After welcoming Laurel Queen back to the winner's enclosure - with plenty of our delighted club members on hand to join in the celebrations at this Saturday fixture - I had to hastily depart with a view to going through the claiming race ritual of the weighing-room wait. Patrick Haslam, as at Edinburgh, was keeping an eye on the situation, obviously anxious to retain Inseyab, owned by his wife. He took the defeat philosophically, commenting: "I don't mind coming up to Scotland again and picking up £600 for finishing second. It's better than leaving the horse in the box at home." No claims were tendered, and I was able to join secretary Pat, and our members, in partaking of the racecourse executive's hospitality. They treat winning owners very well at Ayr. For the Inseyab duo of Patrick Haslam and Kevin Darley, there was winning compensation supplied by Magic Secret in the final event. I wouldn't say that Ayr's hospitality was a major inducement in determining that Laurel Queen returned there later in July. But I felt fairly confident that another post-race celebration lay ahead as we motored up to Ayr for a Friday evening fixture. After her seven furlongs success, Laurel Queen was competing over a mile in the Ayrshire Post Chatline Claimer. John Carroll travelled on to ride her in Ayr's second event after an afternoon stint at Carlisle, where he had to settle for finishing placed on Jack's horses, Oyston's Life and Margaret's Gift. With Laurel Queen in such fine form as she sought a four-timer, and fifth win of the season, the bookies were getting in a meaner mood. She started 11-10 on, and it wasn't easy to beat that price and get evens on the racecourse. Only two of the other five contestants could be given any kind of chance...the 3-1 joint second favourites, Princess Maxine and Claudia Miss. The bookies went 25-1 Clair Soleil, 33-1

Imhotep, 100-1 Supreme Court.

Princess Maxine had gone on from her third-placed run against
Laurel Queen and Inseyab at Ayr to score for the Linda Perratt
stable on a quick reappearance at her home venue. Princess
Maxine's win was achieved at the chief expense of Rahif,
trained by Mary Reveley, whose stable was subsequently to
house the winner. Mary was now opposing us with Imhotep,
who turned out to be a good pacemaker. It was a really hot gallop set by Darren Moffatt's mount, with Laurel Queen and
Claudia Miss going in pursuit as Supreme Court dropped out
of contention. Princess Maxine, held up on this occasion, was
also brought along by Jo Fanning to make a challenge. John
had Laurel Queen taking over from Imhotep with two furlongs
to go, and kept her galloping in great style to hold Princess
Maxine by threequarters of a length. There was no special significance attached to this race. The prize money was
poor...only £1,523. This might make an owner think that racing is run solely for the benefit of bookmakers. But try telling
that to a bookie who has just been hit by a hot favourite like
Laurel Queen. I think the truth must rest somewhere in the
fact that there are too many racehorses in training, too many
owners, too many jockeys, too many trainers, too many race-
courses, too many bookmakers...all seeking a slice of the cake!
But although the Ayr prize money for this claimer was tri-
fling...hardly enough to pay Laurel Queen's training bill for a
month, and Jack Berry is not that expensive... John Carroll
punched the air in delight as he past the post.

We had urged Laurel Queen through that final furlong as if
she was contesting a classic. No thought of monetary gain in
such a moment of sweet success. While waiting for Laurel
Queen to be led into the winner's enclosure, secretary Pat
asked Jack: "Did this win have some special significance for

John.  I've never seen him punching the air like that when he's won a race?"

"No," replied Jack.  "It's just that John loves her."  Didn't we all!  For a horse to take you into the winner's enclosure four times on the trot is absolutely tremendous.  As our ecstastic club members had photographs taken with their heroine, I slipped off to keep an eye on matters claiming.  Linda Perratt and the owners of Princess Maxine offered congratulations as we waited for the "all clear."  There was no problem, although the Ayr collecting box for claims was to become a focal point in a controversial situation involving us at a later date.  I was able to report back to our party that there was another no claims bonus.  Then it was more cheers for Laurel Queen as the Ayr executive once again invited us to "have a drink."

With a winning trip to Edinburgh followed by two successful Ayr ventures, the journey home from Scotland seemed to be getting shorter all the time!  But things went the other way, and in more ways than one, when we made an ambitious southern challenge with Laurel Queen in her next outing.  It's a tidy trip from Lancashire to the glorious venue of Goodwood in Sussex.  To go there and back on a summer Saturday with the holiday season in full swing, and motorway hold-ups inevitable, is just about the worst way I could think of spending a hot sunny day.  The "Racing Post" said that Laurel Queen was the horse travelling the longest distance that day...over 270 miles from Cockerham to Goodwood.  Laurel Queen proceeded to turn in a display that suggested she was suffering from horsebox-lag.

The claimer staged at Goodwood's big meeting is traditionally an extremely competitive event.  This time, Richard Hannon seemed to be holding all the aces, and from an entry of three,

Photo 1a; Sunbathing racegoers see Laurel Queen and Pat Eddery prove a winning partnership at Yarmouth.

Photo 1b; Laurel Queen looking proud of herself in the Yarmouth winners enclosure as Pat Eddery prepares to weigh in.

1

Photo 2: Mel Brittain presents the race trophy to Andrew Heel, fellow racer Jane ... [illegible]

Photo 3; Mike Cropper (right) welcomes Laurel Queen to the winners
enclosure at Thirsk (Gary Carter on board).

Photo 4a; Mark Normington, Cheryl Lister and Raymond Lawson in the No 1 spot with Laurel Queen, at Carlisle.

Photo 4b; Alex Greaves had to settle for second spot on Laurel Queen in the Catterick Handicap, led in by member John Carpenter.

Photo 5: Laurel Queen and John Carroll prevail ahead of Yonge Tender (far side) and Majed in a tight finish at Beverley.

5

Photo 7a; Laurel Queen and John Carroll in command at Edinburgh.

Photo 7b; A Scottish welcome from Charlie Barr, John Reid and John Shedden for Laurel Queen at Ayr.

Photo 8a; John Carroll drives home Laurel Queen to a Rothmans Series success at Newcastle.

Photo 8b; All smiles from members in the Newcastle winners enclosure including club members Ian Nicol and Steve Jones.

Photo 9a; Gordon Russell and John Armstrong in the Ayr winners enclosure.

Photo 9b; Proud member Bill Clennell introduces his granddaughter Anna to Laurel Queen at Newcastle.

Photo 11; It's easy for Laurel Queen and John Carroll in their third Edinburgh success.

Photo 12a; Southwell success for the Laurel Queen fan club.

Photo 12b; A delighted Don White leads in Laurel Queen at Beverley with
Martyn Tattersall following.

Photo 13: Laurel Queen leaves her Lingfield rivals trailing.

13

Photo 14. Jewel Queen romps up the Lingfield hill for her record breaking 22nd win, ridden by Richard Quinn.

Photo 15; A smiling Maisie Shaw leads in the record breaker, with amongst others, club members Joan Wayland and Ian Grant, with a beaming Andrew Hoyle at the rear.

Photo 16a; Mary Reveley nearly became Laurel Queen's trainer over jumps.

Photo 16b; Geoff Lewis who trained Plan Ahead to pip Laurel Queen for the Channel Four Trophy.

he elected to be represented by Knight of Mercy. Meeting the opposition on considerably better than handicap terms, Knight of Mercy looked a Goodwood banker and started 11-8 on. Although not the force of old - in 1990 he had pulled off the Wokingham Stakes and Stewards' Cup double - he had shown with a placed run in Newmarket's Bunbury Cup (when rated 102) that he remained a very useful performer. In a line-up of eight, Laurel Queen was fifth choice in the betting at 11-1. I thought she was worth a sporting each-way bet, although feeling that Knight of Mercy would have to be below-par for Laurel Queen to win.

John Carroll's services were required for his stable's Thirsk runners giving Gary Carter the chance to renew acquaintance with Laurel Queen. Never really travelling well from the off, our filly matched strides with Knight of Mercy early in the straight, then began to back-pedal. As John Reid brought the Hannon horse home ahead of Domicksky and Majal, the fading Laurel Queen finished last. Gary Carter said that she had been outclassed. I couldn't go along with that. Outclassed by the winner, maybe. But the fourth, fifth, sixth and seventh horses should not have outclassed her. Horses don't hold peak form for ever, and it was possible that after the exertions of her winning four-timer, and long haul to Goodwood, she had "gone over the top."

I wanted to hit the long trail home, but had to hang around and ensure that Laurel Queen was not claimed. I was amused by one claim, put in by trainer Rod Simpson, for the runner-up, Domicksky. Rod had kicked up a fuss after having one of his horses claimed earlier in the season. He talked about people "hiding in buckets" then popping out to make claims. He added that he would rather be shot, than claim a horse. Yet here he was going with the flow. It was all right with me because he hadn't claimed MY horse!  That just about sums up what claimers are all about!

# CHAPTER 12

## MAJED CAPTURED

The inquest verdict on Laurel Queen's below-par running at Goodwood was "an off-day." I talked over the situation with Jack and he took the view that we should give Laurel Queen another race before thinking that she might have gone off the boil. There was an attractive claiming race opportunity at Ayr on the Saturday following her Goodwood flop. "I'll give her a quiet week, and if she seems all right, we'll run her at Ayr," said Jack.

On the same day, we had a Haydock claimer picked out for Majed... making his debut in our colours. My admiration for Majed, following his clashes with Laurel Queen at Hamilton and Beverley, had never wavered. Therefore when I saw Majed entered in a Newmarket claimer at a price of £10,000, I thought the opportunity too good to miss. Mary Reveley was running Rahif in the same race. Her son, Keith, was looking after things at Newmarket. I got in touch with Keith and asked if he would mind claiming Majed for me. I told Keith that Majed had little chance of winning because the Newmarket going was much too firm. "But wherever he finishes, claim him," I requested. I watched the 10 furlongs claimer on SIS and saw Majed finish unplaced behind his stable companion, Bowden Boy, the 9-2 favourite. Later in the afternoon Keith phoned to say that he had claimed Majed. Mary Reveley was in Ireland at the time. On her return, I recommended giving Majed a rest until the ground was easier. And I wanted him to have something "in the tank" for a winter campaign over hurdles.  Mary agreed that he would benefit from a break, and after being claimed on June 26, he was making his debut in our colours at Haydock on August 8... his race coming 45 minutes before Laurel Queen's Ayr event.  I decided to travel up to Ayr, while secretary Pat attended the more near-at-hand Haydock meeting.  The weather was very dull, with rain seemingly threatening, when I arrived at the course about two hours before our race.  I spent the afternoon with an anxious eye on the clouds - fearing that rain could scupper Laurel Queen's chance.

It was pouring down at Haydock, but while that would be in Majed's favour, I feared he may not be forward enough to win after his break of about six weeks.  Majed's event was much stronger than the average claimer.  Part of the Juddmonte-sponsored series, it had attracted the 1989 Cambridgeshire winner, Rambos Hall.  Majed was accompanied in the line-up by stablemate, Able Lassie, who was expected to go well.  With the ground in his favour, however, Rambos Hall was able to win readily in the hands of David Nicholls.  Majed was never able to get in a blow at the leaders, but he was making some late headway under John Lowe's guidance in finishing fifth, about 6½ lengths behind the winner.  I was happy enough with this initial effort for us.  And the form was to work out well, Rambos Hall returning to Haydock and taking the Juddmonte Final, then winning the Cambridgeshire again.  And Majed was to prove a real star turn for us, both on the flat and over hurdles.  The rain was continuing to hold off as I waited impatiently for Laurel Queen's event.  We had a new jockey on board in Richard Hills, who had opened the proceedings with a popular success on John Dunlop's even-money favourite, Visto Si Stampi.

Although Laurel Queen had only six opponents in the Darvel

Claiming Stakes, this was a very tricky looking contest. Would Laurel Queen be able to bounce back after the Goodwood disappointment? The question mark against her was a reason for the bookies pricing her at 4-1. Her old rival Mbulwa-out to follow up a Newcastle handicap win-led the market at 3-1. Another "mate," Princess Maxine, was offered at 6-1.

Out to run his rivals into the ground was Mary Reveley's Rahif, but he was a spent force fully three furlongs out. Laurel Queen went on, and briefly raised hopes of providing reasons for sampling more Ayr hospitality. But she was conceding 9lb to Mbulwa, and that made the difference between victory and defeat as a determined Jimmy Fortune urged his mount into a threequarters-of-a-length advantage at the post. As Laurel Queen had finished four lengths clear of the third-placed Euroblake, I felt that she had run close to her best form. Richard Hills said that he had hit the front a little sooner than anticipated when Rahif folded up, but there didn't seem any need for excuses.

When I phoned Jack the following day - only a week after the Goodwood inquest - the talk was of looking for an opportunity that might provide Laurel Queen with a sixth win of the season. That would keep us well in contention for the Channel Four Trophy, which we had missed so narrowly the previous season. Where should we go next? Ayr, of course! I was beginning to think this course was laying on the claimers specially for Laurel Queen. The next one on the agenda was the seven furlongs Burns Claiming Stakes, on August 20. This particular week was certainly something to look forward to, with Laurel Queen in action on Thursday, and Majed contesting a claimer at Chester on Saturday. We wanted dry conditions at Ayr, and the more mud the better at Chester. There was no such luck! The weather forecast indicated there would be rain around in many places during the week. The official report from Ayr was: "Good to soft." When the overnight declarations came through, I was optimistic that Laurel Queen could win - whatever the weather!

The opposition included regular rival Princess Maxine, well held on form. There seemed no threat from Heaven Liegh Grey, a former Berry-trained horse now running for Mark Johnston. I couldn't see Kinlacey, a recent all-weather winner at Southwell, kicking any sand in our faces here. Diet would be pushed to stay seven furlongs. And the other two runners, Bee Dee Ell and Patience Please seemed to pose no problem. Laurel Queen's event was the fourth on the card. By that time, Jack had weighed in with a success by Another Episode in the sprint claimer. I should have taken it as an ominous sign when Another Episode's connections needed to have their wits about them to react in time with a friendly claim when somebody attempted to claim their winner. But we did always keep a close watch on the claiming scene whenever Laurel Queen was involved.

Gary Carter was back on board Laurel Queen and I joked with him that we expected some improvement compared to Goodwood. There's many a true word...Laurel Queen proceeded to turn in one of her most impressive displays...and on soft-ish ground, too!

As Laurel Queen was somewhat slowly into her stride, Gary allowed her to settle in the rear, with Diet doing the pacemaking. After making headway on the bit to lead about 1½ furlongs out, Laurel Queen sprinted clear and the race was all over. Gary was able to ease here up near the line, and at this advanced stage of the campaign, it was heartening that she could win without having a hard time. Laurel Queen had thus equalled her previous season's score of six, and recorded her 15th victory in three seasons. A smiling Gary reported that she had been brilliant and never gave him an anxious moment. Laurel Queen seemed to like Ayr, and we were also getting addicted to winning there. Everything had gone so smoothly, I could ALMOST have forgotten this was a claimer, and that any celebrations needed to be put on hold.

# CHAPTER 13

## SAVILL'S THREAT TO SUE

The "Sporting Life's" northern correspondent, James Lambie, wrote a piece warning that millionaire racehorse owner, Peter Savill, regarded Laurel Queen as a threat to his hopes of retaining the Channel Four Trophy, awarded to the owner of the horse with most wins in a season. That was prior to Laurel Queen's latest Ayr success. Thus when I saw Lambie hanging around in the vicinity of the Ayr claiming box it did not require Sherlock Holmes-type deduction to assume what might be afoot. It was elementary! Lambie was to get his story and a better one than he could have visualised.

Laurel Queen's six wins in the previous season equalled those of Savill's horse, Sense of Priority, but the prize went to him by virtue of a superior record of places. If Savill was looking over his shoulder at us along the 1992 Trophy trail, we were more concerned about keeping tabs on Geoff Lewis's Plan Ahead. My friendly claim was already made out...and for an amount that I felt would ensure Laurel Queen remained with us.

In due course, a brown envelope was popped into the claiming box. I didn't recognise the person putting in the claim. It wasn't Peter Savill. He was in the Cayman Islands. It was the signal for me to tender my friendly claim.

When the claim forms were opened, mine was for the higher amount and my instant reaction was of extreme delight. With people crowding round - Lambie among them - I couldn't see the claiming forms for myself. The news was conveyed to me that we had "won." Someone said that the unsuccessful claim was put in by Peter Savill. Then I was even more delighted. I recall commenting: "Savill will have to come up with more money than that if he wants Laurel Queen." The clerk of the scales then said that the other claim was invalid. I asked him the reason and he said that the form was signed in Peter Savill's name, but had been put in by someone else. This was not allowed. Delight can soon turn to annoyance. The situation meant that an invalid claim had cost us money. The clerk of the scales said that he could not do anything about it. "If it was a frivolous claim, I could refer the matter to the stewards. But it is obviously a mistake," he commented.

It was during these exchanges of words that I said: "You can't tell me that Savill doesn't know how to claim a horse." Lambie included this quote in his "Sporting Life" report and Savill took exception to it, although I didn't find that out until three days later. By the time I was reading about "Owner's Fury" in Friday's paper, I was more concerned about Majed's prospects in a Saturday event at Chester. Pat and I had arranged to stay at Chester on Friday and Saturday night. I was praying for rain to soften up Chester going that was reported to be "good to firm." The weather forecast indicated there would be rain overnight, but when I peeped out of the hotel window on Saturday morning it was dry. Rain began to threaten during racing, but it failed to materialise before Majed's event. The ground was too firm to back him, but he ran a good race, coming from the rear to take third place behind Silver Samurai and Causley. Pat was excited about Majed's running. I was apprehensive about him turning in such a promising performance in a claimer.

Before I arrived at the weighing room I was told: "There is a claim in, but it's not for your horse." Very nice to have your card marked like that. No other claim was tendered, so Majed was retained without me having to sweat. Incidentally, the rain did arrive, an hour too late - just in time to soak everyone leaving the course after the last race. I reflected that Majed would have been a certainty given more suitable ground. Very annoying, considering that he was an 8-1 chance. He proved the point next time out by winning a better event at Haydock on good to soft going. Compensation came at 15-2.

We returned home via a Sunday visit to Chester Zoo. Horses and hippo's all come alike to a true animal lover! But after arriving home, we hardly had time to feed the cat before our son, Ian, was telling us that Peter Savill had been on the phone from the Cayman Islands...threatening to sue us! He had left a number to call him when we returned. When I rang, some-one else answered, and said that Mr Savill would call us back. He duly made the call, and explained that he was very unhappy about some of the things I had been saying about him after the claiming race at Ayr. He then made reference to the news-paper quote: "You can't tell me that Savill doesn't know how to claim a horse." I replied that I was prepared to stand by that quote. It meant exactly what it said: That he knew full well how to claim a horse. Savill could not dispute that - he had claimed enough horses to know the rules. He then stated that he was a lawyer by profession, and that he had grounds for tak-ing legal action against me. "You were saying derogatory things about me after the race, and I will subpoena witnesses to substantiate that." I replied that having been a journalist for many years, I was not in the habit of leaving myself open to allegations of slander, either by what I wrote or said. I added that in the light of James Lambie's "Sporting Life" warning, that Savill was considering putting in a claim for Laurel Queen, I expressed my delight that this attempt had been thwarted. Otherwise, my comments, after the claims had been opened, were directed at "the system," whereby a void claim had cost us money, Savill then explained how the claiming "cock-up" came about. "I asked the bookmaker Alex Farquhar to arrange it. He asked Linda Perratt to put in the claim. I assume that she didn't want to upset me by not putting in the claim, neither did she want to claim one of Jack Berry's horses." Savill said that he had previously told Linda Perratt that he was considering having a horse trained by her. She didn't want to jeopardise the opportunity, yet how could she claim a horse from Jack Berry? The way out was to ask Charlie Williams, who formerly trained at Perratt's Cree Lodge Stables, to do the claiming. The "hot potato" didn't rest easily in Williams' hands, however, because of the liability factor. He didn't want to sign a claiming race form that made him liable for the ten grand. As "liability" is such a corner stone of law, I'm sure that Savill would appreciate his point. At the end, I was the only one liable to cough up any loot. The phone call made by Savill to Farquhar, Scotland's top on-course bookie, who trades under the name, Macbet, turned out to have an expensive outcome - to my company! I had made no mistake, but was left to foot the bill. That was my beef. I fully appreciated that Savill meant to claim the horse according to the rules and that the attempt became subject to human error. As the Ayr clerk of the scales said: "It was a mistake." Savill said that he had not wanted to claim Laurel Queen because she was a threat to his Channel Four Trophy chance. "It will not be the end of the world if I don't win it," he said.

What had annoyed him was that I entered the horse for £9,000 - not the top price of £10,000. But I was only trying to give Laurel Queen every possible chance of winning by taking weight off her, pro rata to the claiming price. And what is £1,000 in terms of racehorse valuation?

I once offered John Dunlop £1,000 profit on a horse he had bought back at the sales for £3,000, and he said: "A thousand pounds profit"...as if I had offered him 10 pence! I upped the profit to £2,000 but there was nothing doing. I bet the horse's previous owner wouldn't have minded the profit. It had cost him over £200,000.

Under the claiming race system at that time, a "friendly" claim, when successful, meant that 10 per cent of the published claiming price, plus 85 per cent of the amount above that figure, had to be paid to the course. We had to pay 10 per cent of £9,000 (£900), plus 85 per cent of £2,025 (£1,721.25) a total of £2,621.25. Deducting the winner's prize money of £1,740 left us with the balance to pay of £881.25.

Savill agreed with me that a revision of claiming race rules was required. I wrote to the "Sporting Life" on these lines and stressed that I had never doubted Savill's claim to have been made in good faith. I wrote to the Jockey Club on this subject and received a reply to the affect that a revision of claiming race rules was in the pipeline. Savill also wrote to the "Sporting Life," recommending a switch to the American system, whereby horses are claimed before the race.

The Jockey Club did bring in changes shortly after the start of the 1994 flat season, but they have done nothing to convince me that things are any better. Some of the problems under the new rules could have been predicted. Either there will have to be more rule changes, or these races will continue to be surrounded by controversy. After all the fun and games at Ayr, we kept Laurel Queen - and ourselves - well away from the claiming scene in the next venture.

# CHAPTER 14

## QUEEN BEATS HANDICAP HOODOO

All those who wrote off the "Queen" as one to ignore in handicaps made a king-size mistake. The faithful were rewarded with an 11-1 touch in the Rothmans Royals Challenge Handicap, at Newcastle.

This 18-runner event, over seven furlongs, came nine days after the fun and games of the controversial Ayr claimer. During that time the claiming race debate had continued - mainly centring on the need for rule changes. To give us a rest from taking the calculated risks that claimers involved, we decided that Laurel Queen's bid for her seventh win of the season would be made in a handicap. And her scintillating form shown in winning so smoothly at Ayr suggested that she would be hard to beat in northern handicap company. The event we chose was better than the average handicap. It was open to horses rated 0-90, and as a "qualifier" in the Rothmans-sponsored series, was sure to be very competitive.

Although 18 runners stood their ground at overnight declaration time, I had already crossed several of them off, as either out of form, or unfavourably handicapped. A rival in cracking form was Flashy's Son, who had won an apprentices' handicap at Redcar only three days before. Cleverly placed by Middleham trainer Micky Hammond, Flashy's Son was now seeking his fifth successive win in handicap company. Having completed the four-timer with the greatest of ease, Hammond was out to strike again while the iron was hot. As racing fortunes were to work out, the Newcastle event could have been lost for Hammond's horse a couple of days earlier at Edinburgh. When Peter Easterby's apprentice, Steve Maloney, won on Thornton Gate in an Edinburgh handicap his claim was reduced from 5lb to 3lb. That could have made all the difference when Steve and Flashy's Son battled out the Newcastle finish with John Carroll and Laurel Queen.

Pessimistic punters had taken the view that although Laurel Queen had 15 wins to her credit, she had never managed to get her head in front when contesting a handicap. This made her very easy to back at around 12-1 in a most appropriate (for Newcastle) "wideopen" betting event.

Just before declaration time, Jack Berry rang me in case I wanted to withdraw and look for an easier option, bearing in mind that we sought a seventh win on the Channel Four Trophy trail. "We must run at Newcastle, I think we're in with every chance," was my reply.

Of the opposition, I though that Mary Reveley's Sharpalto had too much weight, even though partnered by a 7lb claimer. We had the beating of Mbulwa, Super Benz, Jalmusique, Allinson's Mate and Spanish Verdict. I thought that Desert Splendour, trained by Clive Brittain, had a chance on best form. King Al looked weighted out of it with 10st. But there had to be plenty of respect for the bang-in-form Flashy's Son, still carrying only 7st 10lb after such a successful run. Flashy's Son started 6-1 favourite with Laurel Queen, who went off an 11-1 chance, looking wonderful value as an each-way proposition to finish in the first four. Over the straight seven furlongs, Flashy's Son was soon holding a prominent position, with Laurel Queen towards the rear. After disputing the lead, Flashy's Son went on at the furlong marker, with

Laurel Queen improving. It was at this stage that I expected the "out of form" horses to drop away. That happened, and with John getting a good run on the inside, the race was now a two-horse affair. With about half-a-furlong remaining, I thought that Flashy's Son was going to hold off Laurel Queen's challenge. But with John persevering, and Laurel Queen sustaining the effort, the battle was won in the last 50 yards as Laurel Queen nosed ahead and then snatched victory by a neck, with the third-placed King Al four lengths adrift, and Desert Splendour fourth. When a smiling John steered Laurel Queen into the winner's enclosure - to the cheers of an enthusiastic bunch of Laurelites - he exclaimed: "She was certainly game! We had it all to do towards the finish. I think a mile is a better trip for her nowadays."

In the reports of Laurel Queen's latest success in the racing press, I was misquoted as saying: "We hadn't considered Laurel Queen good enough for handicaps." What I DID say was: "Laurel Queen has never had any luck in handicaps." I was referring to handicap attempts such as her seasonal debut second to Colossus at Beverley, when denied a clear run. And to the times when encountering unsuitable ground conditions, as at Edinburgh in 1991 when requiring a Channel Four Trophy clinching win.

The Newcastle triumph kept us in the "Channel Four" running for a second time. Laurel Queen had beaten her previous season's score of six. Would seven wins do the trick? Not that we had finished yet. There was two and a half months of the season remaining and Laurel Queen had kept going until October in her previous campaign. We would be looking for another opportunity in a handicap. But when asked by a racing press representative if I would be likely to run her in claiming company again, I said this couldn't be ruled out, adding: "We would have to think carefully about how much we put her in for. But, after we have done that, if somebody makes a claim that beats our friendly claim, then there are simply no grounds for complaint. We all know the rules when we enter claiming races."

Laurel Queen had not only beaten her handicap bogey, but had achieved it at the chief expense of a horse out to go nap in handicap company. This time she was favoured by the scales just tipping her way. That 2lb lost by Steve Maloney when he won at Edinburgh two days before, could have made the difference in Newcastle's tight finish. I have seen a lot of nonsense written about handicaps. They can be won by a donkey off the right mark, just as too much weight will stop a good horse. At this stage of Laurel Queen's career, it could be said that in giving 9lb and a beating to Flashy's Son - with 16 handicappers in the rear - she had turned in her best performance. How much had it taken out of her? That was something we had reason to reflect upon in her remaining two runs that season.

Next stop was another "Rothmans" handicap on Doncaster's St Leger day card. We were already thinking of starting Laurel Queen's 1993 campaign at Doncaster...in the Lincoln. She was now competing over the round mile, whereas the Lincoln is run on the straight course. But it might as well have been a crooked mile for all the encouragement that Laurel Queen gave us for a return in the Spring. She was never in the hunt as Indian Slave came home ahead of Croft Valley and State Dancer. With John easing her off, Laurel Queen past the post last of the 19 runners. It was terribly disappointing that she had turned in no kind of a show. John said: "She was never going well, and when I asked her to improve her position there was no response. So I let her come home in her own time in case there was something wrong."

Jack took the view that she might have had enough for the season: "We'll give her an easy time for a few days, and I'll get the vet to look her over.  Then we'll see if she ought to have another race."

When I checked with Jack as to Laurel Queen's well-being during the next week or so, the response was encouraging.  With the incentive that another win might clinch the Channel Four Trophy, we decided to enter her for the Chalk Jade Handicap at Newmarket on Cambridgeshire day.

The meeting opened on Wednesday, September 30, with good going.  There was rain around, and it was in the balance whether Laurel Queen would have ground conditions in her favour at the weekend.  Others sweating on whether the Saturday going would be suitable included Mary Reveley.  Like us, she wanted fast ground for Mellottie, who was out to complete a Cambridgeshire double.  Praying for rain was Jeremy Glover, another Cambridgeshire double seeker with Rambos Hall.  It was raining heavily as we drove down to Newmarket on Saturday morning, and whatever the fate of Laurel Queen, I came to the conclusion that Mellottie's Cambridgeshire chance had been washed away and that Rambos Hall must now be the one to back.  When we stopped for "elevenses," I rang up for a price on Rambos Hall and snapped up 6-1.

On arrival at Newmarket, we were told that there had been substantial rain overnight.  Laurel Queen's seven furlongs event was extremely competitive with 29 runners - only one less than the Cambridgeshire.  Fifteen minutes before her race, I saw Goodwood's opening apprentices' event on SIS, and it was X-certificate stuff as Plan Ahead, partnered by Brian Russell, won her seventh race of the season.  Laurel Queen and

Plan Ahead were now on level terms for wins, with Geoff Lewis's horse in the lead when places were taken into account. Any hopes of a quick reply by our filly were left well down the Headquarters course. It was a display nearly as dismal as at Doncaster as she was left toiling while two other Northerners, the 25-1 chances, Hob Green and Gant Bleu, dominated the finish with virtually only the bookies cheering them on. I had feared the worst on the soft ground, but John returned to say: "She wasn't showing any sparkle, but I wouldn't blame the ground conditions. She's going in her coat and is probably ready for a rest." In between Doncaster and Newmarket, Laurel Queen had been taken out of races at Ascot and Newcastle because of soft going. Now we were reluctant to call it a day, with the Channel Four Trophy still up for grabs, but we decided it would be the wisest course.

Whether or not the rain had put a damper on Laurel Queen's Newmarket chance, it did me some good via Rambos Hall, who sluiced to a clear-cut Cambridgeshire success after being backed down to 9-2 favourite. We had already decided that, rain, snow, or blow, Laurel Queen would take her chance in the 1993 Lincoln. Jack said: "She usually comes to hand early, and it would be a great way for her to start the season."

As for the Channel Four Trophy, we had to bow to Plan Ahead as a worthy 1992 winner. Cleverly place by Geoff Lewis, the daughter of King of Clubs followed her Goodwood success by notching an eighth win of the season in an October handicap at Ascot.

# CHAPTER 15

## LINCOLN CHALLENGE

In between spending the winter of 1992-93 dreaming of Laurel Queen winning the William Hill Lincoln, we were able to enjoy some great jumping action by courtesy of our novice hurdler, Majed. This success was not exactly anticipated because when he had been asked to school over hurdles at home, Majed didn't want to know. Peter Niven thought that things might be much different on the racecourse, and that proved to be the case. Sometimes you can know too much! We didn't back Majed in his first hurdles run in our colours, but he hacked up at Ayr, justifying favouritism. Punters plumped for him on the strength of his smart flat form during the latter part of the season. He went on to win a novice hurdle at Haydock, made a successful return to Ayr, and took what was then Kelso's most valuable event, the Hennessy Supreme Novices' Hurdle. He was entered for the Lincoln, but we would only have considered running him if ground conditions came up muddy. Other than on a testing track, a mile trip would be too tight for Majed. The Lincoln was Laurel Queen's race, and, about a month before, Jack was reporting her "going great guns."

The plan was that Jack would assess whether Laurel Queen required a Lincoln warm-up outing on the all-weather, at Southwell. Trying to wind me up, Jack said: "I'm thinking of entering her for a Southwell claimer. How much should I put her in for, £8,000?"

Jack was just awaiting publication of his second book, "A Year

in Red Shirts," and I asked him if he wanted to live long
enough to write a third. We looked like being kept on tenter-
hooks until the eve of the Lincoln to find out if Laurel Queen
was in the line-up. Only 24 could run. The next 24, in handicap order, went into the William Hill Spring Mile. Despite the
early reports of Laurel Queen's well-being, she was not to
reach the Lincoln with a trouble-free preparation. About three
weeks before the race, Jack rang to say she was not right. "I'm
sure it's nothing serious, but she's stiff and I can't gallop her.
I'll send her swimming. That will keep her ticking over, and
she might be all right in a week or two." From then on I was
receiving swimming news, from Settle, rather than cantering
reports from Cockerham.

The improved Southwell run had been ruled out but Jack took
that route to the Town Moor with his other Lincoln entry, Cee-
Jay-Ay. Laurel Queen was duly given the go-ahead to take her
chance, but we feared that she must be short of peak fitness.
At least, we managed to get into the Lincoln line-up, but only
by courtesy of a couple of trainers forgetting that declaration
time was two days before! While Laurel Queen was just above
the cut on 8st, Cee-Jay-Ay stormed home in the Spring Mile at
25-1. We were left wondering, would he have won the Lincoln?
Cee-Jay-Ay had turned in a less than inspiring prep run at
Southwell, but the outing had obviously brought him on a bun-
dle. We had a bumper attendance of members for the big day,
and Jack waved them all into the parade ring. I had a modest
ante-post wager on Laurel Queen at 33-1. The intention had
been to play up the bet, but her disrupted preparation had put
me off further involvement. I was content to be on at more
than double the odds seen on most Doncaster boards. John
Carroll was at his lightest in doing 8st 2lb, putting up 2lb over-
weight. There had been a great debate as to whether the
Doncaster draw would favour the far or near side. Laurel

Queen was drawn No. 7 and Jack said: "We will just have to hope the far side turns out the place to be."

Predictably, the field split into two groups, with Laurel Queen finding the far side pace a bit hot. On the stands side, Golden Chip was setting the early gallop.

With two furlongs to go, High Premium was ahead of Laurel Queen's group, and galloping on strongly. Kieran Fallon kept High Premium going to win from Mizaaya and Will of Steel, with Ringland fourth. Running on strongly in the final furlong, Laurel Queen took fifth place, ahead of Beware of Agents. To finish fifth of 24 after her problems during the three weeks before the race was a fine effort. We were thrilled even though we had just missed out with our each-way bets.

Laurel Queen's return to action had indicated there would be more wins to come. And John jumped off her to assert: "We will just have to come back and win the Lincoln next year." Laurel Queen was in such good heart on her return home that Jack considered entering her for a Rothmans Royals Series Handicap at Lingfield on the following Saturday.

However, the race was on the all-weather track, and Jack though she might not like the surface. In two previous Southwell all-weather runs, Laurel Queen had not been seen at her best. So we waited for a turf event at Pontefract 10 days later. A strong race it turned out to be, too, attracting some very useful handicappers in a line-up of 13.

The bookies were going 11-2 the field, with Leif The Lucky and Hob Green joint favourites. John came into the Ponte parade ring to report: "She's been working really well since the Lincoln." I had already backed Laurel Queen each-way at 7-1.

John's confidence nearly encouraged me to top-up the bet. But what horses do on the home gallops and on the racecourse is often like chalk and cheese.

This was to prove one of the occasions when chalk prevailed. The writing was on the wall early in the Ponte straight after Laurel Queen had made a brief effort to join the leading bunch. She was soon back-pedalling as Leif The Lucky went on to land the spoils from Cool Luke and Pay Homage. "Just not firing today," John reported. "We'll give her an easy few days, before coming to any conclusions," Jack said, adding: "She seems all right." My view, expressed to members before the race, was: "I don't think she likes Pontefract." Now I was even more sure of it. And Jack thought that I might well be right. We would be crossing Ponte off Laurel Queen's list in future. But as far as the Club is concerned, all was forgiven when Surrey Dancer subsequently carried our colours to a 9-1 Ponte success. We can be bought - at a nice price! With Laurel Queen giving Jack the right vibes during the next two weeks, we decided that she should have a crack at Ascot's Insulpak Victoria Cup.

I always regard the Victoria Cup as likely to be a stronger event than the Lincoln. It is staged over a furlong less, but Ascot's straight course is stiff. After Laurel Queen's Pontefract flop, she was now a 25-1 chance in a field of 22. John Carroll was at Ascot to ride Jack's two-year-old, Miss Amy Lou, in the Garter Stakes. He couldn't do Laurel Queen's mark of 7st 9lb, and Lindsay Charnock came down from the north for the one ride. It would be extremely difficult to arrange a more open handicap than the 1993 Victoria Cup. How often do the bookies go 11-1 the field on the day of the race? We had Efharisto, Millsolin, Hob Green, Euro Festival and Risk Master joint favourites at 11-1. But not one of the market leaders could get into the frame. Laurel Queen gave us a good run for our money, leading on the stands rails until approaching the final furlong. At this stage of her career, it was the policy to keep the blindfold on Laurel Queen until all the runners were enstalled. She invariably needed the blindfold before she could be put in the stalls. When Lindsay whipped off the blindfold, Laurel Queen was out of the stalls like a shot. She wasn't fading at the furlong marker - just being beaten for pace! She was only tenth, but a respectable four lengths adrift of the 16-1 chance, Tender Moment, who beat Kayvee, Indian Slave and Little Rousillon. Lindsay was enthusiastic about the way that Laurel Queen had run, commenting: "It was a hot handicap, and she's sure to win more races for you. I was easy on her in the last furlong when her chance had gone."

Jack was well satisfied with Laurel Queen's display. He went off to saddle Miss Amy Lou, who had to settle for fourth place behind Richard Hannon's Wajiba Riva, emphasising that Ascot races are rarely easy to win. At least Laurel Queen was back to form. Or was she?

# CHAPTER 16

## RECORD IN SIGHT

"The race came too soon," is a familiar phrase on the Turf! While it can pay to strike while the iron's hot, many a horse has been beaten by failing to produce peak form in a quick reappearance.

We fell into this trap with Laurel Queen in asking her to contest a Doncaster handicap only five days after the Victoria Cup. She had seemed alright on returning to Cockerham so we decided that she should fulfil a Bank Holiday Monday engagement on the Town Moor. Laurel Queen started at 7-1 in the seventh event on the card, but seven was not to prove a lucky number. However, by that time most punters had benefited from some fairly predicable results. After the first two races went to favourites, Jack's Doncaster specialist, Amron, did his stuff - and at the nice price of 11-2. I happened to be looking for a new club horse to be trained by Geoff Lewis. And when Martina won the claimer, I decided to put in a claim. My claim of £8,005 turned out to be successful, and Martina (trained by John Warton) duly joined Geoff Lewis by courtesy of a horse box supplied by another Epsom trainer, Philip Mitchell. Martina was obtained with the intention of winning a couple of minor events and she achieved that objective with successes at Ripon and Bath.

Amron had won with usual partner, Nicky Carlisle, on board. John Carroll had to settle for third place on Another Episode in Martina's race. But John reached the Doncaster winner's enclosure via the John Gosden - trained Lower Egypt before donning our colours.

What a disappointing end to an otherwise eventful and interesting day it turned out to be! To say that Laurel Queen was never in the hunt would be the best way to sum up a lack-lustre display that my form book described as "lifeless." She trailed in last of nine, as Buzzards Bellbuoy beat Philip Mitchell's Master Hyde by a short head. The most obvious explanation for the flop was that the race came "too soon" after Ascot.

We gave her the best part of three weeks before running her again. A handicap at Catterick was chosen, even though I was apprehensive about her weight, and the likelihood of soft going. But after talking over plans with Jack, it was decided there was little to lose. If she was beaten again, we would look for a claiming race opportunity to get her back in the winning vein. John Carroll was required to ride at Newmarket and Jack suggested that Laurel Queen should be partnered by the "Queen of Sand," Alex Greaves, who was riding work for his stable at that time. The Southwell sand specialist now found herself on muddy ground that would hardly be ideal for Laurel Queen. Under the circumstances, our mare did well to finish a four lengths runner up to Tawafij, who was receiving 10lb. My form book now made the optimistic observation: "Hinted at a return to form here. Hard to beat in claiming company." If that was a hint that we ought to put her back in a claimer then the form book compilers were not to be disappointed. After all, Laurel Queen was still without a win this season, and it was late May! We would have to take drastic action to end the drought. Jack has described winning races as being like a drug. We certainly needed a fix. It was just over three weeks after the encouraging Catterick run that Laurel Queen returned to claiming company at Edinburgh. The going was good and we couldn't really see a particular "danger" horse among her eight rivals in the seven furlongs Leith Claiming Stakes. Everything was right, with the exception of the race distance. A mile would have been more favourable. But John would be happy to set a strong gallop on her if there was a lack of early pace. John found himself with a lead when Diet set the gallop. John had Laurel Queen in close attendance and took up the running at the half-way stage. There was no danger after that with Laurel Queen galloping on in great style to win by 1½ lengths from Obsidian Grey. When I walked into the racecourse betting shop shortly before the race, the SIS commentator was saying that Laurel Queen looked the part in this claimer after running so well in a big handicap like the Victoria Cup.

Punters in general shared that view, resulting in Laurel Queen starting a heavily-backed favourite at 21-20. We were now very much back in the old routine - and I'm not referring to winning! It was the claiming scene again, and I had already filled out the form for a "friendly" claim...just in case! Unfortunately, our hopes for a "no claims bonus" were dashed. A brown envelope was submitted by someone, and mine followed suit. We were able to retain our heroine, but the claim had cost us the prize money of just over £2,000, and a bit more! This race did turn out to have something of a bonus attached to it. As far as claimers were concerned, it was Laurel Queen's swan song. I said to Jack: "No more claimers. Secretary Pat will go mad if we put Laurel Queen in another one." I thought that Jack might be more afraid of Pat than of me. The Edinburgh form worked out well, with the third and fourth horses going on to win. We were keen to see Laurel Queen seeking a follow-up and found an ideal opportunity at Carlisle 10 days later.

Faced with only two opponents in the Carlisle Race Club
Stakes, this looked easy meat. But what looked such a simple
task inevitably revived memories of Laurel Queen's 5-1 on
reverse at the Cumbria venue two years earlier. And the trainer of the one that beat us, Denys Smith, was now opposing with
Media Messenger. The betting was 9-2 on Laurel Queen, 15-2
Media Messenger and Hand On Heart. If any confidence-
booster was needed, it was supplied when Shalabia - a well-
beaten fourth to Laurel Queen at Edinburgh - took the previous race on the card. Laurel Queen kept the form flag flying
high by making all the running under John Carroll's guidance
to beat Media Messenger by six lengths, with Hand On Heart
a further dozen lengths adrift. When you get a rare gift race
like this, its nice to have it all wrapped up and in the bag. At
our club "open day" at Cockerham earlier that month, Jack had
told members: "I think it would be a good idea to retire her at
the end of the season."

With the Edinburgh and Carlisle wins under her belt, Jack
was now having second thoughts. We would certainly miss not
having Laurel Queen in racecourse action after all the exciting
times she had brought for us. We hadn't stumbled on such an
easy opportunity at Carlisle by accident. While things couldn't
have gone more in our favour at declaration time, to leave only
three runners, the conditions of the race were tailor-made for
Laurel Queen. We had already found another attractive opportunity for her at Catterick on July 14. That was three weeks
away, and we decided to enter her for a Leicester handicap and
assess the strength of the opposition. The seven furlongs was
not ideal, but we allowed her to take her chance, and it nearly
came off. John attempted to make all the running, but Pat
Eddery brought Superoo with a strong run to lead in the final
furlong and score by a head. Superoo, trained by John Sutclffe,

had been out of form, but first-time blinkers did the trick.

In an open 11-horse handicap, Laurel Queen (the 9-2 favourite) had turned in a good effort. We now looked forward to her contesting the Layburn Limited Stakes at Catterick. John thought that she would have won at Leicester had the distance been a mile. She had won over the Leicester mile as a three-year-old. But although she would be competing over seven furlongs at Catterick, the conditions of the race put her in with every chance. There was drama five days before the event when only three entries were made and the race was nearly scrapped. Fortunately, a phone call from the racecourse to the respective trainers brought assurances that the three entries would run, and the race was given the go-ahead. We were in the sixth event on a seven-race card, and with rain falling throughout the afternoon, I was getting more worried by the minute. I thought that 4.30 would never come! There was some respect (not mine) for Laurel Queen's rival Sylvan, but the other runner, Gentle Hero, had not raced for some time and was 12-1 outsider. Laurel Queen edged favouritism at 6-5 on, with Sylvan a 5-4 chance.

There was nothing close about the race. Looking in tremendous shape in the parade ring, Laurel Queen provided the only anxious moment when rearing and performing a rodeo act at the start. Once in the stalls, she was quickly out of them, and proceeded to make all the running. Well clear in the final two furlongs, John was able to ease her down and beat Sylvan by eight lengths. This smoothest of successes enabled Laurel Queen to equal the British mainland record of wins by a filly or mare in post-War years. With her career tally now standing at 19, our task was to find the right events in which Laurel Queen could become the clear-cut record holder. Much studying of the Racing Calendar lay ahead.

# CHAPTER 17

## QUEEN'S SPRINT SUCCESS

Some students of racing form may have been surprised when we elected to run Laurel Queen over six furlongs at Southwell. All her 19 wins had been achieved over either seven furlongs or a mile. Jack Berry was at first vehemently against running her over six furlongs at this advanced stage of her career. But having found an ideal winning niche for Laurel Queen, to get her away from claimers, I considered that a six furlongs opportunity was too good to miss.

After being forced to make a friendly claim to retain Laurel Queen following her first win of the 1993 season, at Edinburgh, we found the newly-instituted "Limited Stakes" events a godsend. Laurel Queen just managed to get into the 0-70 range, staged over seven or eight furlongs. Her win at Carlisle had been achieved in the Race Club Stakes for horses rated 0-75. Then the first Limited Stakes chance came for her at Catterick.

An easy win whet my appetite for seeking further Limited Stakes success with Laurel Queen, and I wasn't put off when I saw two such races coming up, although both were over six furlongs. It would be a matter of choosing between them because there was only an interval of two days at Doncaster (Thursday) and Southwell (Saturday).

When I suggested to Jack that we enter for both, and then weigh up the respective opposition, the groan, received in response, had been anticipated. But despite his attempts to make me change my mind, I refused to budge. The next day, Jack called on John Carroll to try and persuade me to re-think about running Laurel Queen over six furlongs. John could tell I wasn't going to change my mind, but after reporting back to Jack, he made a second attempt. I stressed to them both that I had no intention of trying to turn Laurel Queen into a six furlongs handicapper, and didn't want her to go for something like the Ayr Gold Cup. My reasoning was that if the opposition was significantly inferior, Laurel Queen could even win over five furlongs. The point was eventually conceded, and Laurel Queen thus entered at Doncaster and Southwell, the latter being a turf fixture. When I saw the Doncaster entries, I didn't fancy Laurel Queen taking on Samsolom, who had run into some fine form for Surrey trainer, Peter Howling, and won three off the reel. I rang the Howling stable and found out that Samsolom was a certain runner. That made up our minds...it was Southwell here we come!

Samsolom won the Doncaster race very easily, and the starting price of 9-4 was better than expected. We backed him, of course. If Jack still had any lingering doubts about the six furlongs trip as the runners paraded at Southwell, they were not shared by Laurel Queen's partner, Gary Carter. We had a strong representation of Laurel members at sunny Southwell, and most of them made their way into the parade ring, although they didn't stay there for long when the jockeys came out.

"What do you think about her chance, Gary," said Jack. "I think she's a certainty," was Gary's ultra-confident response. You should have seen those club members shooting off in the direction of the betting ring. They bolted faster than some cauliflowers I once attempted to grow.

Laurel Queen moved even more speedily after a smart exit from the starting stalls. Gary was able to dictate throughout and bring Laurel Queen home an eased-down 2½ lengths ahead of Mindomica. As that was her 20th success, it could be said that Laurel Queen had broken the record for the number of wins by a filly or mare in post-War years. The mare Misty Halo held the record with 21 wins, but two of them were achieved in the Isle of Man. It could be questioned whether the Manx wins should count. But Jack and I wanted there to be no argument about Laurel Queen being the record-holder. So as far as the Southwell celebrations were concerned, we settled for Laurel Queen having broken the mainland record.

This initial six furlongs success by Laurel Queen attracted media attention, but I was mainly pleased because we had taken another step towards establishing her as the undisputed record holder. My only jibe at Jack was to say: "I wonder if we ought to move her up to 10 furlongs next?" I honestly think that she would have stayed a mile and a quarter.

While I could claim that this Southwell victory was down to me steering her in the right direction, an earlier win on this course came about purely due to Jack's opportunism, without me having a chance to intervene. That was when Laurel Queen pulled off a double at Edinburgh (Monday) and Southwell (Friday). She recorded what I regarded as a hard-fought success at the Scottish track and consequently I was shocked when Jack declared her for the Southwell event only four days later. But he produced her looking like new paint to record one of the most impressive wins of her career. Laurel Queen's Southwell successes were both achieved on turf. She did make two "all weather" appearances at Southwell, but they were unsuccessful. Her first run on the sand came at the end of her juvenile campaign when she was "over the top." We then put her away for the season. She also contested a Southwell all-weather event as a three-year-old, but after finishing unplaced, was found to be stiff in her hind quarters. Thankfully, a rest put her right.

We had a sponsored race night coming up at Lingfield on Saturday August 7. The event we supported was the six furlongs Laurel Racing Club Handicap Stakes. We would have a big attendance of members there. What better way could we entertain them than by running Laurel Queen? And surprise, surprise...the card just happened to include what we now looked upon as one of Laurel Queen's own races...a Limited Stakes! We had the right race. Now all we required - with a visit to Geoff Lewis's Epsom stables arranged for the Sunday morning - was a fine weekend. And we couldn't have done better in the Bahamas! It was a brilliant weekend, both weather and winner-wise. Lingfield provided us with a marquee, equipped with a bar, but it was an evening for being outside basking in the sunshine. Laurel Queen's event was the last on the card, but well worth waiting for even though she seemed sure to start odds-on favourite. John Carroll was travelling on to Lingfield after an afternoon stint at Haydock. Laurel Queen was his only evening ride, but expected to reward him with his 14th win on her. He was in the winning vein, having scored at Haydock on Jack's sprint handicapper, Gorinsky.

As the six runners were about to be enstalled for the seven furlongs Metropole Limited Stakes, the commentator referred to Laurel Queen as "this fantastic filly from the north who needs one win to equal the record for a filly or mare in post-War years." She had remained steady in the betting market at 7-4 on, with Charmed Knave (out to follow-up a Leicester success) second favourite at 9-2. Laurel Queen's No. 1 draw would have been a worry in a bigger field, but John was able to get her away really well, and then move over to the stands side. It was plain sailing as John brought her home an easing-down four lengths ahead of Charmed Knave, trained by David Laing, who had won our sponsored race with My Ruby Ring. Laurel Queen was the fourth Lingfield favourite to oblige, so plenty of punters must have gone home with pockets well-lined. After reporting to us that the race had been as straightforward as it had seemed from the stands, John Carroll was hitting the trail back to the north. Laurel Queen would soon be heading that way in her horse box. For Pat and I there was an overnight stay for the open day at Geoff Lewis's Thirty Acre Barn Stables. Special guest at Geoff's was the triple Grand National-winning hero Red Rum. If all the packets of Polo Mints that Red Rum has crunched his way through in a life time were stacked on top of each other that would make an obstacle that even Liverpool's most famous leaper couldn't have negotiated in his prime. All he had to do at Geoff's - apart from eating Polos - was jump onto the scales for a "guess his weight" competition.

Our club horse with Geoff, sprinter Martina, had contributed to a good month by preceding Laurel Queen's Lingfield success with August wins at Ripon and Bath. We had dropped Martina in class to contest a Ripon seller, and only managed to retain her after Mr Colin Tinkler Sen, took an interest and helped to push the bidding up to 7,200 guineas. We were anxious to retain Martina because there was an ideal follow-up opportunity at Bath. Martina was 13-8 favourite when Pat Eddery partnered her to a Ripon victory over Brisas, but she was a 6-1 chance when Paul Eddery snatched a short head verdict on her at Bath, where she had to overcome a difficult No. 16 draw in a field of 19. Given a low number in the draw, Martina would have started at much shorter odds.

As we travelled home following the weekend at Lingfield and
Epsom my thoughts were very much of Laurel Queen requiring
one more win to become undisputed record holder. And with
five wins behind us in the 1993 season - after a six and a seven
in the two previous campaigns - we were once again among the
leading contenders for the Channel Four Trophy.

# CHAPTER 18

## HASLAM CLASH - THE REVENGE

Patrick Haslam had to settle for place prizes in two claiming race clashes between his filly, Inseyab, and Laurel Queen, but he found the right horse to beat her in a Hamilton handicap. Our mare looked high in the weights on 9st 11lb in the Scots Guards Handicap, over Hamilton's extended mile, but there was no "easy" option following her 21st win. It was disappointing when the overnight declarations numbered seven. I would have preferred eight to make Laurel Queen an attractive each-way proposition. Hot favourite was the Haslam-trained Talented Ting, who was seeking a four-timer and still looking on the right side of the handicap. Talented Ting's winning roll had started with an unchallenged eight lengths victory over No Comebacks on the Hamilton course towards the end of July. A 5lb penalty was then defied at Nottingham. So our horse certainly appeared to have plenty to do conceding 8lb to such a bang-in-form performer. As the Nottingham distance was 1¼ miles, the same jockey, Kevin Darley, would be making plenty of use of Talented Ting on reverting to a mile.

Talented Ting was 5-4 market leader, with Straw Thatch, who could be regarded as a winner without a penalty, second favourite, at 4-1. Then it was 9-2 Laurel Queen, 5-1 Mentalasanythin. Straw Thatch had been disqualified and placed last after winning a handicap at Ayr. He didn't require the stewards' intervention to finish last here. Straw Thatch was never in the hunt as Talented Ting set the gallop. Laurel Queen was moved up to get on terms with half-a-mile to travel, but always seemed to be struggling. Kevin Darley was able to settle the issue at the furlong marker, and although Mentalasanythin mustered a late threat, Talented Ting had threequarters of a length to spare, with Laurel Queen three lengths away in third place. We had to feel satisfied that Laurel Queen had acquitted herself well in this 0-80 handicap. On such an occasion there's always a bright side: "Maybe the handicapper will drop us a pound or two," said Jack.

John reported: "I kept asking Laurel Queen to find a little bit, but each time she responded, Kevin was always finding an answer to us." It was obvious that the task of conceding 8lb to Talented Ting was too tough. Jack stressed that she was a shade too high in the handicap. He had to dash off to saddle Palacegate Touch, whose task looked considerably easier in the following claimer. The "Touch" was landed, but only at 9-4 on in a three-horse contest.

Laurel Queen took the Hamilton outing in her stride and we entered her for a seven furlongs handicap at Redcar the week after. I was apprehensive about the venue. She had an unfortunate experience there as a two-year-old, and later turned in a below-par effort in a claimer. But easy pickings were not to be found at this stage of the season. We might as well let her run, rather than spend the day looking out of the stable door.

Sometimes, what seems to be a difficult race when the entries are published, can become dramatically easier due to drop-outs at overnight declaration time. We had experienced such "bonuses" along the way. But nothing happened at Redcar declaration time to make us regard Laurel Queen's task as any easier.

I'm not superstitious so it was the quality of the Redcar rivals, rather than the fact the field numbered 13, that worried me. Mary Reveley was running two. Amazing Feat and Parliament Piece. I thought that we had the beating of Parliament Piece, who was conceding 11lb. But I had the utmost respect for Amazing Feat even though he was taking a long time to peak in his 1993 season. Laurel Queen had finished well ahead of Amazing Feat in the Lincoln. However, he was now 6lb better off, and judging by his 1992 form, he could be an "autumn horse." Before making my way to the Redcar parade ring, I had seen Laurel Queen priced at 8-1, which was as expected. I had a modest each-way bet on her, more in loyalty, than in confidence that I might collect. She looked on good terms with herself in the parade ring. Jack, John, myself, and club members, all agreed it was a wide-open handicap. Apparently this verdict was not unanimous. Laurel Queen remained at 8-1 "on-screen" when I returned to the stand. Then I could hardly believe my eyes as the odds began to drop until she was 100-30 favourite at the off.

My own explanation for the gamble - when I had time to think about it later - was that the money came for Laurel Queen because of lack of confidence in the other runners. It was the final event on a seven-race card and throughout the afternoon I had not heard of one fancied runner out of the 13. This turned out to be the stage for Amazing Feat to recapture his magic of the year before. Laurel Queen disputed the early lead with Savahra Sound and Parliament Piece, but weakened at the furlong marker. Amazing Feat came through, demonstrating decisive pace, to settle the issue in the hands of Ray Cochrane. North Ardar was a respectable 2½ lengths runner-up, and this performance was one of the reasons that led me to obtain him when he won a Pontefract seller in the following season. Laurel Queen faded into sixth place, which must have been very disappointing to the participants in the substantial punt on her. John said that she had never been travelling all that well, even when in the leading bunch. He wondered if she had "gone over the top." Jack also thought that she might have had enough for the season. I suggested that we let the dust settle, and then review the situation .

I phoned Jack at the weekend and he told me that Laurel Queen seemed to be perfectly happy and that there was no reason why she shouldn't have another race. After all, there was just over two months of the season remaining. "But we won't rush her," Jack said. I agreed, and mentioned a Limited Stakes event at Lingfield in mid-September as an attractive target. "That's her race - all being well," Jack enthused.

Discussing her running at Redcar, I told Jack that the more I weighed up the form of the race, the more I became convinced that she had turned in a much better performance than we had thought at the time. "You could be right," Jack said.

In his final two outings of the season, the Redcar winner, Amazing Feat, beat a stong handicap field at York, and finished second to Henry Cecil's smart three-year-old, Wharf, in the Baring Darley Listed Stakes at Newmarket. Amazing Feat had two runs in between Redcar and Newmarket - one of them on the day that Laurel Queen went to Lingfield in search of the record 22nd win.

# CHAPTER 19

## RECORD CATCH 22

The wait of over three weeks in between Laurel Queen running at Redcar and taking the record trail to Lingfield would have seemed a lot longer but for another interesting development on the club scene. My search for a new horse - preferably a dual purpose performer - led to Surrey Dancer joining our string to be trained by Mary Reveley...with novice hurdling in view. Obtained for £15,000 after finishing third in a claimer at York's early September meeting, Surrey Dancer turned out to be a cracking jumper. And the same could be said for the horse that beat him first time in our colours in a 10 furlongs handicap at Nottingham. We had 8-1 about Surrey Dancer before he was backed down to 7-2 favourite. It was tough luck that a field of 23 included one as good as Mysilv, to whom Surrey Dancer was conceding nearly a stone. With the weight terms more favourable in his next outing at Pontefract, Surrey Dancer was able to compensate us with a 9-1 success. Mysilv was a well-beaten fourth. On the day before, Majed had snatched a short head verdict to justify 5-4 favouritism in a Chester handicap. "We're on a roll," remarked one of our members, Mark Coulthard, in the Pontefract winner's enclosure. These wins came about a month after Laurel Queen's return to Lingfield for her record bid in the Renown Limited Stakes. When successful on the course some six weeks earlier, she had scooted home on fast ground. My big worry now was the weather forecast...indicating that the dry areas were all north of Watford! Weatherwise, the North-South divide was very much in evidence on the day. The Lingfield fixture co-incided with the Ayr Gold Cup meeting. While Laurel Queen liked both these courses, I was wishing that she could have been heading for Scotland rather than the South.

The going at Ayr was fast, while soft conditions prevailed at the Surrey venue. While I won't admit to being superstitious, I do take encouragement from things going favourably on a race day. For instance, I once travelled to Catterick and every traffic light I approached was green. That turned out to be the signal for the two horses we had running that day - Classic Ring at Catterick, and Laurel Queen at Yarmouth - to complete a double!

Apart from my apprehension about the ground conditions as I travelled by train to London, en route to Lingfield, it hardly seemed like a good omen when Euston Station became subject to a security alert. Given another couple of minutes grace, I would have been on the tube heading for my connection at Victoria. It didn't take long to walk over to Euston Square and head for Victoria on an alternative route, but this took me on a roundabout journey - with the tubes packed out.

I had left home at 7.30a.m., thinking that the train journey would save me all the hassle of the M6, M40, M25, etc. I arrived at Lingfield seven hours later having decided that driving a car was a piece of cake, and that BR was definitely not my cup of tea.

It was a soggy Lingfield scene. No wonder the first race winner, Rainbow Heights, was an odds on chance. It was one of those days when they inflict an eight-race card upon you...just about all you don't need after a wearisome journey to the course and the prospect of getting home at midnight...with a bit of luck! Laurel Queen was in the seventh race, and that turned out to be very lucky, indeed. Watching the earlier races staged on the straight course told us that horses drawn high, on the stands side, were running into a patch of boggy ground. David Elsworth's two-year-old, French Gift, took the far side route to victory in a six furlongs event. This told me that Laurel Queen, drawn nine in a field of 11, would have to get over to the other side of the course if she was to have a winning chance.

My belief was confirmed by Sumoto, Queen's View and the pace-forcing Sunday's Hill filling the first three places after racing up the far side in a seven furlongs Conditions Stakes. In between Lingfield events, I visited the course betting shop to keep in touch with happenings at Ayr and Yarmouth. A Beverley card had been called off because of a thunderstorm. The ground was very fast at Ayr, where John Carroll was riding for the three days. John was probably wishing he was down at Lingfield after his well-fancied mount, Frisky Miss, had been beaten by rank outsider stablemate, Zanzara (Jimmy Fortune) in a two-year-old event. But he experienced better luck on Palacegate Jack, who completed a Berry double by pipping Pinkerton's Pal in the Harry Rosebery Stakes. With the Berry horses in the winning vein, and the Lingfield path to victory seemingly sorted out, things were looking up with regard to Laurel Queen. John Dunlop was a visitor to the Lingfield course betting shop, obviously interested in the Yarmouth stayers' handicap in which his Cesarewitch, entry Sun Grebe, was involved.

Sun Grebe was a hot favourite but didn't shine in finishing fourth to Provence. Neither was there any joy for Dunlop with his three-year-old stayer Harlestone Brook, an eight lengths second to Safety In Numbers in the Lingfield handicap preceding Laurel Queen's race. At Ayr, I collected from a winning

forecast when Hi Nod made his weight advantage tell over
Amazing Feat. Things really were on the up-and-up.

Richard Quinn was booked to ride Laurel Queen. He knew all
about the hazards of Lingfield's boggy stands-side having
found that route unfavourable when he partnered Young Ern
in Sumoto's race. He was in full agreement when I insisted:
"Win, lose or draw, the only chance is to get over to the far
side." I added that Laurel Queen wouldn't mind being out in
front if she made a fast exit from the starting stalls. Had this
race been staged during her three-year-old campaign, I would
have written off her chance because of the soft ground. But at
age four and five she became more adaptable.

Now all the racing experience derived by Laurel Queen in her
jaunts over a wide variety of tracks was to be put to a "record"
test. The tension mounts. They're under orders. They're off!
And Laurel Queen is away to a fast start with Richard - like
the rest of the runners - heading for the far side! Laurel Queen
found herself racing just behind Champagne 'N' Roses, ridden
by Michael Roberts. So far, so good! What I didn't want now
was a cut-throat battle for the lead, leaving the way for something else to pick them off. After two furlongs, Champagne 'N'
Roses looked like having to settle for sackcloth and ashes.
Laurel Queen forged ahead resolutely and began to open up a
clear lead. Looking back through the field, the rest of them
were labouring. Laurel Queen and Richard Quinn had run
them ragged. The record was ours as she came home an eased-
down five lengths victor, with Rocality and Mr Nevermind bat-
tling for minor berths. A delighted Richard returned to the
winner's enclosure to give Laurel Queen a hearty slap and
salute her triumph with the appropriate accolade: "She's a
real pro." He added that Laurel Queen had responded to
everything required of her, had gone through the ground real-

ly well, and couldn't have won more convincingly.

What a comeback after Redcar. And what a superbly stylish way to break the record. The Lingfield executive also turned on the style by inviting us to toast Laurel Queen's triumph with a glass of champagne. This was a nice gesture, and members joining me for a drink included Mrs Joan Wayland and her mother, Mrs Dorothy Cochrane, who later travelled with me from Lingfield to Victoria. That left them a "stone's throw" from home, compared to my trip north on a train that toured the Midlands en route to Preston, Lancs.

Jack Berry, and our club members throughout Britain, had been disappointed to find that the Lingfield card was not covered by SIS. The racing at Ayr was over by the time Laurel Queen contested the 5 20. Jack said: "I stayed behind to listen to the race commentary in the betting shop. You should have heard those punters cheering on Laurel Queen - and not just because she was 11-4 favourite. She must be one of the most popular horses of all time."

Interest in Laurel Queen's pursuit of Misty Halo's record had intensified following a "Racing Post" comparison of their respective records in an article by John Randall, early in July. At that time, Misty Halo was leading, 21 to 18. Randall pointed out that Laurel Queen was in joint second place with Granville Greta.

Misty Halo, trained by Sir Mark Prescott, won half of her 42 races, between the ages of two and six, in seasons 1981-85. Superbly placed to such winning effect by her trainer, Misty Halo's successes included a trainers' invitation event at Catterick, when there was no prize money, 11 wins (including two in the Isle of Man) in amateurs' races, and two apprentices' events. Critics will say some of these were soft touches. They say the same about Laurel Queen. But to win a lot of races with a horse, you need to have that Turf adage in mind about "keeping yourself in the best company, and your horse in the worst." John Randall said that the toughness and enthusiasm of Misty Halo made her more of a public favourite than many more talented winners. As Jack Berry pointed out, it was the same with Laurel Queen. Whereas our filly was at her best over seven furlongs or a mile, Misty Halo required a middle distance or more, winning up to 2¼ miles. Granville Greta, who won her races between 1959 and 1965, and raced until a nine-year old, became a very popular sprinter after winning a selling race as a two-year-old. Ernie Davey, an ace handler of sprinters, placed Granville Greta very shrewdly.

We received a letter from the owners of Misty Halo, Mr and Mrs Christopher Philipson, congratulating us on Laurel Queen's success, and reporting that their mare, at the age of 14, was still hale and hearty at stud in Essex, and in foal to Danehill.

In the 1994 flat season, the winning line of Misty Halo was being maintained by her three-year-old daughter, Shifting Mist (by Night Shift), also carrying the Philipson colours and Prescott-trained. Secretary Pat had been unable to attend Lingfield for the record-breaking occasion and she eagerly awaited my late-night return home to watch the race video, presented to me at the course. We'll never tire of seeing Laurel Queen's record-breaking success.

# CHAPTER 20

## "QUEEN" HOPES ARE DASHED

The start of the 1994 flat turf season was about a month away when I took Pat over to the Cockerham stables to see our two-year-old Laurel Diamond. One of our members, Graham Hoof, met us in Cockerham village, to join us in the visit. We were favoured by a fine, if chilly day following a brief spell of bad weather. Snowdrifts, three feet or more, remained along the hedgerows to remind us that winter was not over yet. But we received the usual warm welcome from Jack Berry's assortment of dogs, including Laurel, Hardy, and Jack's favourite, Ollie, on parking up in the yard.

I had to laugh one day at Carlisle, after a win by Laurel Queen, when Jack emerged from the weighing room, followed by his son, Sam, John Carroll...and Ollie, the Jack Russell bringing up the rear. When Jack saw me laughing, he smiled and said: "Ollie certainly gets around."

Later on this particular Sunday afternoon, Ollie was to provide us with some more laughs.

But from the moment we saw Jack-and although the main purpose of our visit was to see our two-year-old colt Laurel Queen took centre stage. "You should see her," Jack enthused. "I've never known Laurel Queen winter so well. She looks terrific! We should have put her in the Lincoln."

Jack was chiding me for having suggested that we give the

Lincoln a miss this time. Laurel Queen had contested the 1993 Lincoln and turned in a fine run in finishing fifth of 24 to High Premium. However, it had been touch and go whether Laurel Queen made the Lincoln line-up.

In deciding against entering Laurel Queen for the 1994 Lincoln, I was put off by the thought of her ending up in the Spring Mile with a big weight to carry, and at the same time haunted by the Cee-Jay-Ay spectre. I had also told Jack that this would take some pressure off both him, and the horse, in the light of the previous year's "will she, won't she" run problems. Having felt happy in the knowledge that Laurel Queen could come to hand in her own good time, as she approached her fifth season of racing, it now seemed that she was going to be all dressed up for Doncaster, but with nothing to do but peer over the stable door.

Jo Berry took us out to look at Laurel Queen...and no wonder Jack was impressed with the mare. She was a picture. After many of Laurel Queen's victories, I've wished I had been photographed with her. But in the excitment of such magic moments, I've usually been too busy chatting to club members, or the racing press about our heroine. With no such distractions as Laurel Queen was paraded before us in the indoor school, my immediate reaction was: "We should have brought the camera."

Jo's response was: "No problem." And off she went to get a camera, and we duly had our photographs taken with a remarkably relaxed Laurel Queen.

To see her looking so lovely, and on such good terms with all around, was something special. While she does usually look well, she can behave like a bit of a madam at times. I gave her

114

a few polo mints, and she gobbled them up, gratefully. Unlike our two-year-old, when we went off to visit him. He declined my offer of a mint, but it was a safe bet that he would be crunching along, just like his older stablemates, in due course. I wonder who are the biggest consumers of mints, humans or horses? Red Rum must be the finest advert that polo mints could possibly have had. If Laurel Diamond was backward in coming forward for a mint, he looked the same way in terms of his racing career. No disrespect meant to the trainer. The colt hadn't grown much since the autumn, and (understandably, considering the wind-chill factor) was clinging on to his winter coat.

As Jo showed us round the 100 plus horse-power team, it was not hard to form the conclusion that many more winners would be coming Cockerham way in 1994. An absentee was our four-year-old sprinting filly, Laurel Delight (Paris House's half-sister), who was at Newmarket being covered by former champion miler, Selkirk.

We returned to the warmth of the kitchen, and while partaking of liquid refreshment, Graham asked the guvnor: "Do you think you can win the Brocklesby, this time." Jack's confident reply was: "I reckon I can." At that early stage, Jack didn't want to elaborate on which one he could win the Brocklesby with. But when Mind Games duly delivered the goods at Doncaster, there was every reason for Graham, yours truly, and all the Laurel punters to be on a first-day-of-the-season winner.

You may have heard of a doggy bag, but probably not one like Jack had acquired for Ollie. Jack explained that intrepid traveller Ollie was making a mess in the car with his dirty feet. Hence the bag. But before Jack could get Ollie's legs into the bag, and zip it up, leaving only his head poking out, a series of circus tricks had to be performed.

Among Jack's many pets was once a Wallaby, until the animal hopped it, never to be seen again. I imagine Ollie would take some catching the next time the "travel bag" came out.

As for Laurel Queen, what had promised to be another memorable campaign in 1994 was suddenly cut short by an injury to a hind leg incurred during a home gallop.

One minute we were looking forward to seeing her attempt to add to her record tally. The next her career was over. Fate had been kind for a long time. Now it was cruel. We couldn't complain after all the wonderful winning moments. Laurel Queen lived on in richly deserved retirement, with no lasting discomfort, that was the main thing.

Stable girl Maisie Shaw, who looked after Laurel Queen prior to moving South to take up a post with Epsom trainer Gary Moore said: "If I could have taken "Queenie" with me, I would - like a shot! I'm a softie, but I was very keen on her and still miss her like mad. I'm proud to have had anything to do with her. She's one in a million!" And so say all of us!

# CHAPTER 21

## STRAIGHT FROM THE HORSE'S MOUTH

I was quite pleased when I heard someone say that I was going to be called Laurel Queen. After all, some horses do have dreadful names. If one of the Arab owners had bought me for two million dollars I would probably have ended up with a name like Mukkerpalmatey. Incidentally, that's Arabic for "user friendly." Ever since the advent of a certain Mr Ed, horses have taken a great interest in language. Yes, we hear a lot of language in the stable yard. And as I was to become aware after making my racecourse debut at Pontefract, there's a lot to be learnt about language during a race. The jockeys don't wrap it up. Not that that nice John Carroll ever swore at me. He just swore at the others! Mr Berry was always very good to me, although a bit stingy with the polo mints.

Other horses in the stable, and a lot of those I met on my travels, have often asked me which was my most exciting race.

I honestly don't know. But I can tell you which was the race that gave me most satisfaction. It was when I won for the 21st time, at Lingfield. I had been feeling sick as the proverbial parrot because the Laurel Racing Club was sponsoring a Lingfield race and I was not allowed to run in it. Something about the stupid race conditions. I'm surprised that Andrew and Pat Hoyle - and all the Laurel Club Members - stood for it. If I had been in the Laurel race, I would have won it, no question about that, and probably at a good price. And yet they had me running in the last race, with everybody saying that I would be odds-on. I was really peeved, and gave serious consideration to becoming a non-trier. Then I decided that the sooner I got past the winning post, the sooner I would be heading back to the comfort of my nice warm bed at Cockerham. So I planned to nip down the Lingfield straight a bit sharply. Then it came to mind how John Carroll had waved his whip in a victory salute after a win at Ayr. Why should I let him steal all the glory? This time, I would give my own victory salute....by flashing my tail!

We duly made all the running to win easily and after passing the post I gave my tail a real good flash. It was great fun. But on returning to the winner's enclosure I heard a racing journalist say that I was ungenuine for flashing my tail. I did my best to kick him, but he managed to dodge out of the way. He was obviously used to avoiding his editor's boot.

Apart from that prat upsetting me, I had liked Lingfield, and when I heard that I would be returning there to seek my record-breaking 22nd win, I was really chuffed. The weather was a lot different though. It was bucketing down, and I knew that Andrew would be worried about whether I could cope with the ground conditions. The number of times I have walked around the parade ring and listened to him moaning: "She won't win on this ground." I suppose I used to be a fussy filly, as a two and three-year-old, but later on I would just take the ground conditions in my stride. While I was walking around the parade ring on this occasion, I heard Andrew stressing to Richard Quinn (some new jockey they had come up with) how I was badly drawn and would have to be taken to the other side of the course as soon as the starting stalls opened.

I thought, what a load of balony! Why don't they include a detour around the car park at the same time! But I knew that

Andrew meant well. He had probably been up all night study-ing the form book. What a waste of time. I had had a quiet word with all the other runners, and found out that none of them felt up to it. Who needs to study form?

On the way to the start I heard a bookmaker shouting: "Eleven to four Laurel Queen". A colt called Confronter, who was in opposition, winked and shouted to me: "You should be eleven to four on, not against".

I think Confronter fancied me. Anyway, he would have a nice view of my hindquarters during the race. That's all the lot of them saw of me. They just weren't up to all the rain and mud.

When I got back to Cockerham, Jack Berry was saying: "I think she's done enough for this season". Great stuff - I was set for a nice long holiday.

Even though Neville, the feedman, dishes up some good fodder, a few days out at grass would be much appreciated. But by the time a new flat season came round, I was always bored and kicking the stable door in readiness for some racecourse action.

You think about getting back in the winner's enclosure at places like Ayr, Edinburgh, Hamilton (I love those Scottish courses), Lingfield, Warwick, Southwell, and those lovely Yorkshire tracks, and the Midlands meetings. Even a slog down to Yarmouth is inviting as a new season approaches.

I won't bore you any more with details of how an injury put paid to all such hopes of me re-visiting all the old familiar places in 1994.

As they say, all good things must come to an end. I'm glad I managed to sneak in that record win at the end of the 1993 season. Saved me from having to race on crutches! Wonder how long the record will stand? I'll just have to produce a filly foal to keep it in the family.

Reserve my old space at Cockerham, Mr Berry .

# LAUREL QUEEN'S RACING RECORD

## Season: 1990 (two-year-old)

July 2nd.

**Pontefract:** Wragby Stakes (Maidens).
Five furlongs. Fourth to Mostimus.
8 ran. Jockey: John Carroll.

July 10th.

**Pontefract:** Monkhill Auction Stakes
(Maidens) (Division II). Six furlongs.
Third to Bijoux D'Or. 10 ran. Dist. 3
lengths, neck. SP 5-2. Jockey: John
Carroll.

July 18th.

**Yarmouth:** Harrison Selling Stakes.
7 furlongs. Won from Green's
Enterprise and Zamina. 11 ran. Dist. 2
lengths, 1½. SP 11-10 fav. Jockey: Pat
Eddery.

July 24th.

**Redcar:** Fine Leg Selling Stakes. 7 fur
longs. Unplaced to Kagram Queen. 11
ran. Jockey: John Carroll.

August 31st.

**Thirsk:** Mel Brittain Selling Stakes. 7
furlongs. Won from Friday Fourball and
Jolizal. 15 ran. Dist. 2½ lengths, 1. SP
7-2. Jockey: Gary Carter.

September 11th.

**Carlisle:** Greylag Claiming Stakes
(Division I): 7 furlongs: 4th to
Station Express. 12 ran. J Carroll

September 19.    **Yarmouth:** Norfolk Farmers Claiming Stakes. 7 furlongs. Won from Lady Baraka and Hideaway. 14 ran. Dist. One length, 5. SP 6-1. Jockey: Gary Bardwell.

October 1st.    **Wolverhampton:** Oaken Lodge Nursery. 7 furlongs. Fifth to Maggie Siddons. 17 ran. Jockey: John Carroll.

November 7th.    **Southwell:** Blackbird Claiming Stakes (Division I). 1 mile. Unplaced to Samta Grai. 18 ran. Jockey: John Carroll.

## Season: 1991 (three-year-old)

April 2nd.    **Warwick:** Kingswood Claiming Stakes Division I). 7 furlongs. Won from Bid For Elegance and Pesidanamich. 11 ran. Dist. Short head, 5 lengths. SP 11-2. Jockey: John Carroll.

April 19th.    **Thirsk:** Knayton Selling Stakes. 7 furlongs. Fourth to Yonge Tender. 15 ran. Jockey: John Carroll.

April 26th.    **Carlisle:** Kestrel Claiming Stakes (Division II). 7 furlongs. Won from Daazam and Nishcor. 9 ran. Dist. 10 lengths, ½. SP 11-4. Jockey: John Carroll.

May 6th.    **Doncaster:** Bawtry Claiming Stakes. 7

furlongs. 19 ran. Third to Fizz Time. Dist. 1½, 1½. SP 5-1. Jockey: John Carroll.

May 20th.      **Hamilton:** Beeshill Claiming Stakes. 1 mile, 40 yds. Won from Dust D'Throne and Stairway to Heaven. 10 ran. Dist. 7 lengths, ½. SP 11-8 fav. Jockey: John Carroll.

May 30th.      **Carlisle:** Levy Board Apprentice Stakes 1 mile. Second to Hickory Wind. 4 ran. Dist. 2½ lengths. Jockey: Wally Hollick.

June 27th.      **Carlisle:** BBC Radio Cumbria Fillies' Claiming Stakes. 6 flgs, 206 yds. Fifth to Annaceramic. 15 ran. Jockey: John Carroll.

July 20th.      **Southwell** (Fibresand): NPT Handicap (3-year-old only). 1 mile. Unplaced to Hazar. 11 ran. Jockey John Carroll.

August 24th.      **Newcastle:** Gallowgate Claiming Stakes. 1 mile. Fifth to Stairway to Heaven. 13ran. Jockey: John Carroll.

September 16th.      **Edinburgh:** City Cab Fillies' Claiming Stakes. 1 mile. Won from Sharp Money and Miss U Like Crazy. 14 ran. Dist. 3 lengths, 1. SP. 4-1 co fav. Jockey: John Carroll.

September 20th.

**Southwell:** East Midlands Electricity Claiming Stakes. 7 furlongs. Won from Unanimous and African Chimes. Dist. 2 lengths, 1½. SP 5-1. Jockey: Nicky Carlisle.

September 23rd.

**Nottingham:** Carlton Claiming Stakes. 1 mile, 54 yds. Unplaced to Lord Oberon. 20 ran. Jockey: Gary Carter.

October 16th.

**Wolverhampton:** Go All Weather Claiming Stakes. 7 furlongs. Second to Brown Fairy, Caromish third. 16 ran. Dist. 2 lengths, 3½. SP 15-2. Jockey: John Carroll.

October 29th.

**Leicester:** Fosse Way Claiming Stakes. 1 mile. Won from Genuine Lady and Tohamah. 19 ran. Dist. 3 lengths, sh.hd. SP 4-1 joint fav. Jockey: Gary Carter.

November 7th.

**Edinburgh:** Tennents November Handicap. 1 mile. Unplaced to Languedoc. 15 ran. Jockey: John Carroll.

## Season 1992 (four-year-old):

March 27:

**Beverley:** Withernsea Handicap. 7 flgs, 100 yds. Second to Colossus, with Euroblake third. 14 ran. Dist. 1½ lengths, 1½. SP 10-1. Jockey: John Carroll.

April 9th.              **Hamilton:** Standard Life Handicap. 1 mile, 65 yds. Fourth to Majed. 8 ran. Jockey: Gary Carter.

April 23rd.           **Beverley:** Brian Boyes Claiming Stakes. 1 mile, 100 yds. Won from Yonge Tender and Majed. 16 ran. Dist. sh.hd and same. SP 5-2. Jockey: John Carroll.

May 7th.               **Carlisle:** Buttermere Claiming Stakes (Division I). 1 mile. Fourth to Just A Step. 10 ran. Jockey: Lindsay

Charnock.

June 1st.               **Redcar:** Ian Herd Claiming Stakes. 7 Flgs. Unplaced to Ringland. 12 ran. Jockey: John Carroll.

June 25th.            **Carlisle:** BBC Radio Cumbria Fillies' Claiming Stakes. 7 flgs. Won from Spanish Performer and Ravecino. 7 ran. Dist. Hd, 8 lengths. SP 6-1. Jockey: John Carroll.

July 18th.             **Ayr:** Cambeltown Claiming Stakes. 7 furlongs. Won from Inseyab and Princess Maxime. 4 ran. Dist. Hd, 3½. SP 6-4 fav. Jockey: John Carroll.

July 24th.             **Ayr:** Ayrshire Post Chatline Claiming Stakes. 1 mile. Won from Princess Maxine and Claudia Miss 6 ran. Dist.

¾ length, 2. SP 10-11 fav. Jockey: John Carroll.

| August 1st. | **Goodwood:** Turf Club Claiming Stakes. 1 mile. Unplaced to Knight of Mercy. 8 ran. Jockey: Gary Carter. |
|---|---|
| August 8th. | **Ayr:** Darvel Claiming Stakes. 1 mile. Second to Mbulwa, with Euroblake third. 7 ran. Dist. ¾ length, 4. SP. 4-1. Jockey: Richard Hills. |
| August 20th. | **Ayr:** Burns Claiming Stakes. 7 flgs. Won from Heaven Liegh Grey and Kinlacey. 7 ran. Dist. 2 lengths, 1. SP 9-4 fav. Jockey Gary Carter. |
| August 29th: | **Newcastle:** Rothmans Royals Challenge Handicap. 7 flgs. Won from Flashy's Son and King Al. 18 ran. Dist. Neck, 4. SP 11-1. Jockey: John Carroll. |
| September 12th. | **Doncaster:** Rothmans Royals Handicap.1 mile (round). Unplaced to Indian Slave. 19 ran. Jockey: John Carroll. |
| October 3rd: | **Newmarket:** Choke Jade Handicap. 7 flgs. Unplaced to Hob Green. 29 ran. Jockey: John Carroll. |

## Season 1993 (five-year-old)

March 27th.     **Doncaster:** William Hill Lincoln Handicap. One mile (straight). Fifth to High Premium. 24 ran. Jockey John Carroll.

April 6th.     **Pontefract**. Landbridge Shipping Handicap. One mile. Unplaced to Leif the Lucky. 13 ran. Jockey: John Carroll.

April 28th.     **Ascot:** Insulpak Victoria Cup Handicap. 7 flgs. Unplaced to Tender Moment. 22 ran. Jockey: Lindsay Charnock.

May 3rd.     **Doncaster:** Sandall Beat Handicap. One mile (round). Unplaced to Buzzards Bellbuoy. 9 ran. Jockey: John Carroll.

May 22nd.     **Catterick:** Rothmans Handicap. 7 flgs. Second to Tawafij with Ballad Dancer third. 7 ran. Dist. 4 lengths, 1½. SP 8-1. Jockey: Alex Greaves.

June 14th.     **Edinburgh:** Leith Claiming Stakes. 7 flgs. Won from Obsidian Grey and Nutty Brown. 9 ran. Dist. 2½ lengths, ½. SP 21-20 fav. Jockey: John Carroll.

June 24th.     **Carlisle:** Carlisle Race Club Stakes. 1 mile. Won from Media Messenger and Hand On Heart. 3 ran. Dist. 6 lengths, 12. Sp 2-9 fav. Jockey: John Carroll.

July 5th.            **Leicester:** Scraptoft Handicap. 7 flgs.
                     Second to Superoo, with Tiffanys Case
                     third. 11 ran. Dist. Nk, ½. SP 9-2 fav.
                     Jockey: John Carroll.

July 14th.           **Catterick:** Leyburn Limited Stakes. 7
                     flgs. Won from Sylvan and Gentle Hero.
                     3 ran. Dist. 8 lengths, 6. SP 5-6 fav.
                     Jockey: John Carroll.

July 24th:           **Southwell** (Turf): Raspberry Limited
                     Stakes. 6 flgs. Won from Mindomica
                     and Chilly Breeze. 6 ran. Dist. 2½
                     lengths, 2. SP Evens fav. Jockey: Gary
                     Carter.

August 7th.          **Lingfield:** Metropole Limited Stakes. 7
                     flgs. Won from Charmed Knave and
                     Great Hall. 6 ran. Dist. 4 lengths, ¾.
                     SP 4-7 fav. Jockey: John Carroll.

August 16th.         **Hamilton:** Scots Guards Handicap. 1
                     mile, 65 yds. Third to Talented Ting
                     and Mentalasanythin. 7 ran. Jockey:
                     John Carroll.

August 25th.         **Redcar:** Whitby Handicap: 7 flgs.
                     Unplaced to Amazing Feat. 13 ran.
                     Jockey: John Carroll.

September 16th.      **Lingfield:** Renown Limited Stakes. 7
                     flgs, 140 yds. Won from Rocality and Mr
                     Nevermind. 11 ran. Dist. 5 lengths, hd.
                     SP 11-4 fav. Jockey: Richard Quinn.

# MISTY HALO'S 21 WINS
## 1981

| | | | | |
|---|---|---|---|---|
| 5 Oct | W'hampton | Bushbury Maiden Stakes (Div2) (1m) | C Nutter | £690.00 |
| 19 Oct | Hamilton | Thankerton Stakes (1m 40yd) | G Duffield | £1,098.40 |

## 1982

| | | | | |
|---|---|---|---|---|
| 25 Aug | Brighton | Brighton Ladies' Stakes (1¼m) | Mrs E Mellor | £1,312.20 |
| 20 Sep | Leicester | Gaddesby Apprentice Stakes (1¼m) | A P O'Leary | £1,149.30 |
| 5 Oct | Brighton | Southdown Stakes (Gentleman) (1½m) | Mr R Hutchinson | £1,339.50 |
| 16 Oct | Catterick | Frazer Hines Cup (Gentlemen) (1½m) | Mr J Ringer | £891.60 |
| 25 Oct | Chepstow | Horseshoe Apprentice Stakes (Div 1) (1½m) | K Williams | £1,109.40 |

## 1983

| | | | | |
|---|---|---|---|---|
| 2 July | Beverley | East Riding Yeomanry Challenge Trophy (Amateurs) (2m) | Mrs E Mellor | £958.10 |
| 11 July | Pontefract | Ackton Hall Stakes (1½m) | G Duffield | £1,354.20 |
| 3 Aug | Pontefract | Rotherham Stakes (1½m) | G Duffield | £1,576 |
| 10 Sep | Chepstow | Mademoiselle Ladies' Stakes (1½m) | Miss D Jones | £955.30 |
| 11 Oct | Redcar | Saltburn Stakes (2m 115yd) | G Duffield | £1,203.20 |

## 1984

| | | | | |
|---|---|---|---|---|
| 23 Apr | Nottingham | Nottingham Amateur Rider' Stakes (1m 5f) | Mrs E Mellor | £1,436 |
| 19 May | Castletown | House of Questa Stakes (Amateurs) (2m) | Mrs E Mellor | £414 |
| 17 July | Ayr | Kirkoswald Stakes (1m 5f) | G Duffield | £1,716 |
| 7 Aug | Redcar | McCoy Brothers Stakes (Amateurs) (1½m) | Mrs E Mellor | £1,690.80 |
| 15 Oct | Pontefract | Stayers Stakes (2¼m) | G Duffield | £1,914.80 |

## 1985

| | | | | |
|---|---|---|---|---|
| 18 May | Castletown | Stewards' Cream of the Barley Stakes (Amateurs) (2m) | Mrs E Mellor | £414 |
| 5 Aug | Redcar | Mommessin Stakes (Amateurs) (1½m) | Mrs E Mellor | £1,301.70 |
| 14 Aug | Catterick | Northern Trainers' Invitation Race(1½m 40yd) | G Oldroyd | ---------- |
| 8 Oct | Brighton | Southdown Stakes (Gentleman) (1½m) | Mr R Hutchinson | £1,836.40 |

# LAUREL QUEEN'S 22 WINS
## 1990

| | | | | |
|---|---|---|---|---|
| 18 July | Yarmouth | Harrison Selling Stakes (7f) | Pat Eddery | £2,574 |
| 31 Aug | Thirsk | Mel Brittain Selling Stakes (Div 1) (7f) | G Carter | £2,595 |
| 19 Sep | Yarmouth | Norfolk Farmers Claiming Stakes (7f) | G Bardwell | £2,763 |

## 1991

| | | | | |
|---|---|---|---|---|
| 2 Apr | Warwick | Kingswood Claiming Stakes (Div1) (7f) | J Carroll | £2,521.20 |
| 26 Apr | Carlisle | Kestrel Claiming Stakes (Div2) (7f) | J Carroll | £2,542.90 |
| 20 May | Hamilton | Bellshill Claiming Stakes (1m 40yd) | J Carroll | £2,759.90 |
| 16 Sep | Edinburgh | City Cab (Edin.) Claiming Stakes (1m 16yd) | J Carroll | £2,595 |
| 20 Sep | Southwell | East Mid. Elec. (Mansfield) Claiming St (7f) | N Carlisle | £2,833.30 |
| 29 Oct | Leicester | Fosse Way Claiming Stakes (1m 8yd) | G Carter | £2,975.40 |

## 1992

| | | | | |
|---|---|---|---|---|
| 23 Apr | Beverley | Brian Boyes Claiming Stakes (1m 100yd) | J Carroll | £2,402.40 |
| 25 June | Carlisle | BBC Radio Cumbria Claiming Stkes (6f 206yd) | J Carroll | £2,343.60 |
| 13 July | Edinburgh | Dunbar Claiming Stakes (1m 16yd) | J Carroll | £2,374 |
| 18 July | Ayr | Campbeltown Claiming Stakes (7f) | J Carroll | £2,262 |
| 24 July | Ayr | Ayrshire Post Chatline Claiming Stakes (1m) | J Carroll | £1,523 |
| 20 Aug | Ayr | Burns Claiming Stakes (7f) | G Carter | £2,263.50 |
| 29 Aug | Newcastle | Rothmans Royals Nouth-South Handicap (7f) | J Carroll | £4,077.50 |

## 1993

| | | | | |
|---|---|---|---|---|
| 14 June | Edinburgh | Leith Claiming Stakes (7f 15yd) | J Carroll | £2,460.30 |
| 24 June | Carlisle | Carlisle Racing Club Stakes (7f 214yd) | J Carroll | £2,743.40 |
| 14 July | Catterick | Leyburn Limited Stakes (7f) | J Carroll | £3,199 |
| 24 July | Southwell | Raspberry Limited Stakes (6f) | G Carter | £3,054 |
| 7 Aug | Lingfield | Metropole Limited Stakes (7f) | J Carroll | £3,611 |
| 16 Sep | Lingfield | Renown Limited Stakes (7f 140yd) | T Quinn | £3,598 |

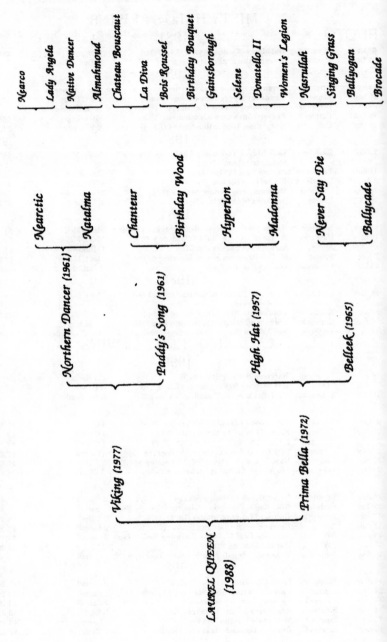

Pedigree of Thoroughbred Laurel Queen

PHOTOGRAPHS; courtessy of, Ken Bright, Robert Elliot, Fotosport(Keith Robinson) Caroline Dunwoody The Evening Statndard and club members.

131

# Laurel Racing Club

**Laurel Queen** wove a winning thread through four memorable flat seasons to bring the wonderful thrill of successful ownership to the many Laurel Club members.

**Fleet-Footed,** a hurdler trained by Mary Reveley, was the club's first winner. While Laurel Queen was compiling her 22 wins, great backing came from **Kestrel Forboxes, Classic Ring, Rose Glen, Majed, Laurel Delight, Martina, Laurel Romeo** and **Surrey Dancer** --- all club winners.

The club's share in Jack Berry's Moss Side Racing Group brought more wins --- from **Doublova, Grand Time** and **Fort Hope.**
**Majed** and **Surrey Dancer** have proved fine club servants both on the flat and over hurdles.

A new venture came for the club with the 1994 covering of four -year-old sprinting filly, **Laurel Delight,** by the former champion miler, Selkirk, and it is planned that the club's breeding interests will be extended to include **Laurel Queen.**

Club winners have been trained by Jack Berry, Mary Reveley, Geoff Lewis, Alan Bailey and Tommy Fairhurst.

Inquiries regarding **Laurel Racing Club membership,** or brochure requests, will be welcomed by the company directors, Andrew & Pat Hoyle, who deal with all matters personally.
> **Phone 01772-734313**
> **Or write to: Laurel (Leisure) Limited**
> **PO Box 198**
> **Preston**
> Lancs, PR2 7ED

## *"Britains Friendliest Racing Club"*